BICYCLE REPAIR
AND MAINTENANCE

BICYCLE REPAIR
AND MAINTENANCE

By Ben Burstyn

arco
New York

This book is dedicated to "Izzy" London, who was my first boss in 1936 and to Oscar Wostyn who I considered one of the best bicycle mechanics in his lifetime.

Published by Arco Publishing Company, Inc.
219 Park Avenue South, New York, N.Y. 10003

Copyright © 1974 by Ben Burstyn

Dec 17 1975
Nov. 26, 1974

Library of Congress Catalog Card Number 72-86242

ISBN 0-668-02706-1 (Library Edition)
ISBN 0-668-02708-8 (Paper Edition)

Printed in the United States of America

Contents

Chapter I

Care and Maintenance of Your Bicycle

KNOWING YOUR BICYCLE

Understanding the functions of the various parts that make up a bicycle will help the owner to maintain the bicycle so that a minimum amount of repairs will be required to keep it in good mechanical condition.

Although there are hundreds of differently shaped bicycles manufactured, they are all basically built so that the rider is seated approximately two-thirds of the distance back from the front edge of the bicycle, and must use his legs and feet to make it move and his arms and hands to steer it.

WHAT SIZE BICYCLE TO RIDE

In order to get the maximum efficiency out of the bicycle, it is important to know how to ride it properly. An ill-fitting bicycle changes pleasure to work. As a result, the rider will soon lose interest in the bicycle or will find another means of exercise or transportation.

First of all, the rider should be in such a position on the bicycle that he will use a minimum amount of effort to ride it. This can be done by having the correct size bicycle for the rider.

Adult bicycles are measured by frame sizes. These sizes can be determined by measuring the height of the frame from the center of the crank axle to the top of the bicycle tube directly under the saddle or seat, as shown in Fig. 1.

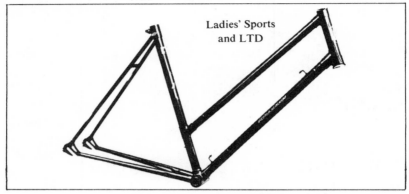

Ladies' Sports and LTD

Fig. 1.   Height of frame.

Although the length of a person's legs is the proper means of determining the size of the bicycle he should ride, the following table can be used for the person of average build:

4'8" to 5'1" _____ 17" to 19" frame
5'1" to 5'4" _____ 19" to 21" frame
5'5" to 5'8" _____ 21" to 23" frame
5'9" to 6'0" _____ 23" to 25" frame
6'1" and up _____ 25" to 26" frame

The higher a person sits on a bicycle, the less he will have to bend his knees. The less knee-bending, the less effort used.

TYPES OF BICYCLES—SINGLE AND MULTIGEAR

As I have mentioned, the moving force of a bicycle is the pedaling of the rider. On a single-gear bicycle, the gear ratio remains the same (one sprocket on the crank and one sprocket on the rear wheel). The only way that another speed can be gotten on this type of bicycle is to change the size of either the crank sprocket or the sprocket on the back wheel. In order to change gear ratios without having to change the size of the sprocket, it is necessary to have a multigear bicycle. Multigear bicycles consist of from two to fifteen or more different gear ratios.

MULTIGEAR BICYCLES

Multigear bicycles have been on the market for over 50 years. There are various combinations of multigears. There is a two-speed coaster brake hub, a three-speed hub without a coaster brake, a four-speed hub, a five-speed hub, a plain hub with clusters of two to six sprockets, and also a two- or three-sprocket unit to fit on the crank assembly.

The most popular adult multigear bicycles are operated with a derailleur. A derailleur (as the word implies) derails the sprocket chain from one sprocket to another. This is what gives the bicycle a different gear ratio. On a five-speed bicycle, there is one derailleur attached to the frame of the bicycle on the right side next to the rear axle. On an eight- or more gear bicycle, there are two derailleurs. One derails the chain at the crank sprockets, and the other derails the chain at the cluster of sprockets attached to the rear wheel.

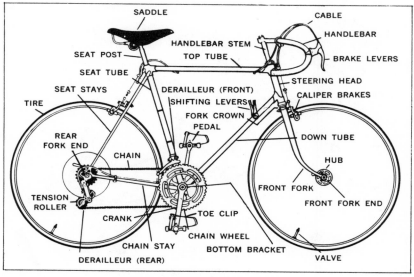

Fig. 2.   Make-up of a bicycle.

The advantage of having more than one gear on a bicycle is that the rider can change the gear ratio while riding so that he can pedal up an incline using the same effort that he would use if he were riding on a level road. He may also increase the speed of the bicycle by putting it in a higher gear, and not have to pedal any faster.

Fig. 3.   Riding positions.

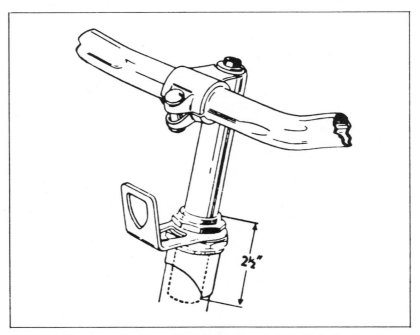

Fig. 4.   Position of handlebar stem in bicycle fork.

MAKE-UP OF A BICYCLE

Starting with the front part of the bicycle, I will explain what each part does to make the bicycle go. In later chapters of this book, I will go into more detail on various types of bicycles and the mechanism used to operate the bicycle.

The following is an explanation of how a bicycle fits together and the various functions of its components.

HANDLEBARS AND HANDLEBAR STEMS

There are a wide variety of handlebars used on bicycles. Most adult multigear bicycles use a racing or "drop" bar. When using this type of bar, the extension of the handlebar stem is important for the comfort of the rider. A person with a large-frame body should have a long extension stem, while a person with a short-framed body should use a stem with a short extension. This way his body will position itself better for a more comfortable fit. On a tourist-type handlebar, the rider is sitting in an almost upright position. To have the most comfortable handlebar of this type, try to get one that is approximately the width of your shoulders. Leaning slightly forward when sitting on the bicycle is less tiring than sitting up straight.

The handlebar is attached to the bicycle by means of a handlebar stem. The stem serves two functions: It keeps the handlebar in the desired up-and-down position, and it also keeps the handlebar at a 90 degree angle to the bicycle frame. The handlebar stem is secured in place inside the bicycle fork by means of an expanding wedge. This prevents the handlebar from turning without turning the fork. A binder bolt at the front of the stem secures the handlebar to prevent any up or down motion while someone is riding the bicycle.

BICYCLE FORK

The bicycle fork is held in place on the bicycle by means of two sets of bearings placed in head cups, one on the bottom and one on the top of the head of the bicycle. The fork has a lower stationary cone and an upper adjusting cone, plus a lock washer and lock nut to keep the fork properly adjusted. The fork is properly adjusted when it turns freely inside the frame and there is no excess play when turning the fork.

The function of the bicycle fork is:
1. To hold the front wheel in place.
2. To hold the handlebar to the bicycle.
3. To allow the bicycle to be steered.

THE FRONT WHEEL

The front wheel of the bicycle is fastened securely to the bottom of the fork with axle nuts and washers. The center of the wheel is called the hub. The hub contains a set of bearings on each end, an axle, a cone on each side of the axle for the bearings to ride on—the cones must be adjusted so that the wheel will spin freely and at the same time not have any side play—two washers, and two axle nuts.

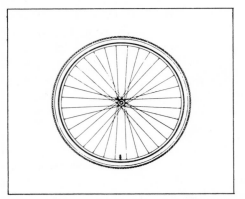

Fig. 5.   Front wheel of bicycle, showing hub.

THE SEAT POST AND SADDLE

Moving back toward the center of the bicycle, an adjustable seat post is fastened securely to the frame of the bicycle (in the desired position) by means of a seat post collar or clamp. The bicycle saddle is fastened to the seat post by means of an adjustable saddle clamp, which is attached to the saddle hardware beneath the saddle.

THE CRANK ASSEMBLY

At the bottom of the bicycle frame, directly below the saddle, is the crank assembly, consisting of crank cups, bearings, cones,

HOW TO ADJUST YOUR SADDLE

HEIGHT. Raise or lower by loosening nut "A". **Be sure that at least 2½ in. of the saddle pillar remains in the frame.**

FORWARD or BACKWARD. By loosening nuts "B" on either side of the saddle its chassis can be moved forward or backwards.

By reversing the clip (as shown on dotted line "C") the saddle can be set further back.

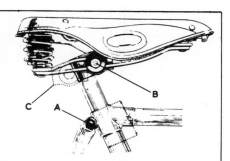

Fig. 6.   How to adjust your saddle.

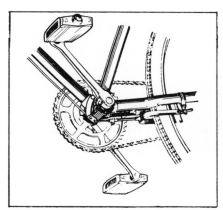

Fig. 7.   Three-piece crank assembly.

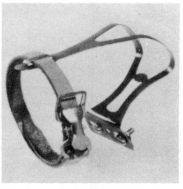

Fig. 8.   Toe clips for riding with less effort.

Fig. 9.   Rear wheel with three-speed hub.

Fig. 10.   Rear wheel with coaster brake.

lock washers, lock nut, crank axle (or "crank" on the American type), crank sprocket, crank arms, and pedals. There are different types of crank assemblies, and I shall go into more detail about them in a later chapter. The function of the crank assembly is to transmit motive power from the rider to the rear wheel by means of a chain connecting the crank assembly to the rear wheel.

TOE CLIPS

Toe clips on the pedals are cage-like devices that are fastened to the pedals in such a way that the rider can put his feet in them when riding the bicycle. With toe clips on the pedals, the rider not only uses his leg power on the down stroke of the crank, but he also uses his leg power on the stroke coming up. This enables him to get more efficiency from his bicycle.

REAR WHEEL

The rear wheel of the bicycle is the driving wheel. It propels the bicycle forward with transfered motive power applied at the pedals, through the bicycle chain to the rear wheel. The rear wheel is fastened to the bicycle at the rear fork stays, and is held onto the bicycle by means of axle nuts and washers.

BRAKING SYSTEMS

There are three different types of braking systems used on bicycles. The coaster brake is a brake fitted in the hub of the rear wheel operated by the rider's feet. Caliper brakes are fitted on the front fork and rear frame below the saddle, and are operated by means of levers and cables or steel rods attached to the handlebar and caliper brakes. They use rubber blocks pressing against the wheel rim to stop it. Drum brakes have a brake lining on brake shoes which press against a drum to make the wheel stop. The drum brakes are operated by hand levers.

This explanation gives you a rather complete picture of the basic bicycle. Naturally, we shall need to know about the different types of braking mechanisms, gear-shifting mechanisms, and the various multispeed rear hubs. In the following chapters I shall go into detail in explaining the function of all the above-mentioned devices that make for a more enjoyable bicycle ride.

Chapter II

Proper Maintenance Means Longer Life

Like any other moving vehicle, the more you understand your bicycle, the less trouble you will have with it. As a bicycle does not require expensive tools to keep it in good operating condition, anyone can afford to care for his bicycle.

TOOLS NECESSARY FOR SERVICING A BICYCLE

1. Bench vise
2. Screw drivers
3. Crescent wrench
4. Metric open-end wrenches #8 through #15
5. Vise grip pliers
6. Regular pliers
7. Tire tools
8. Spoke wrench
9. Flat cone wrenches
10. Patch kit
11. Tire pump

LUBRICATING THE BICYCLE

Every moving part on a bicycle requires lubrication. All ball

lubrication

REGULAR LUBRICATION IS IMPORTANT

Lubricate the parts shown when new and every two weeks when in use. If the cycle has been idle for some time, lubricate before using. DO NOT OVER-OIL. If a gearcase is fitted remove gearcase end and lubricate the chain while revolving the cranks (see page 17).

On some models the Bottom Bracket, Pedals and Hubs do not have a lubricator provided in which case these bearings have been grease packed before leaving the factory, giving lubrication over a long period without attention.

When not in regular use cycle should be hung up to protect tyres. Metal parts should be lightly smeared with grease if storage is for an extended period.

Do not allow surplus oil to run down spokes and ruin tyres.

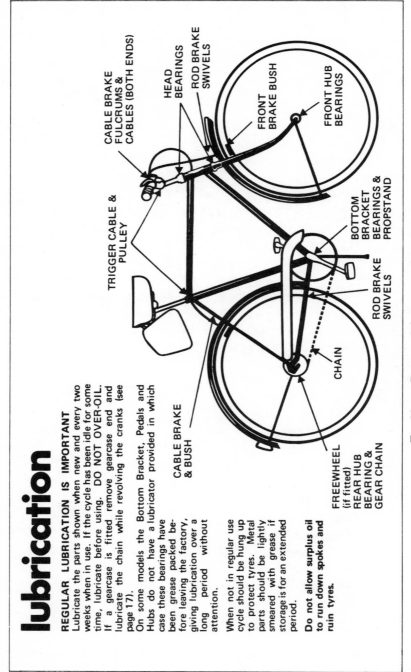

CABLE BRAKE FULCRUMS & CABLES (BOTH ENDS)

HEAD BEARINGS

ROD BRAKE SWIVELS

FRONT BRAKE BUSH

FRONT HUB BEARINGS

TRIGGER CABLE & PULLEY

BOTTOM BRACKET BEARINGS & PROPSTAND

ROD BRAKE SWIVELS

CABLE BRAKE & BUSH

CHAIN

FREEWHEEL (if fitted) REAR HUB BEARING & GEAR CHAIN

Fig. 11.   Points to lubricate on a bicycle.

bearings should be lightly coated with a lightweight cup grease. The places to lubricate are: the front wheel (bearings on each side); the bicycle fork (bearings on top and bottom); the crank assembly (bearing on right and left side); the rear wheel (all bearings). Further instructions on lubricating coaster brakes and three- and five-speed hubs are explained in the instructions on the repair of each particular hub. A few drops of machine oil on the pedals (where they are attached to the crank) will make them last much longer. Some pedals can be taken apart. On this type you can grease the bearings to preserve them. Pedals that come apart usually have an adjusting cone, washer, and lock nut. Make sure when putting the pedal together that the lock nut is tight against the lock washer, and at the same time that the pedal spins freely but does not have any side play. The best lubricant for the bicycle chain is powdered graphite. Cover the chain with a light coat of graphite about once a year. Grease your bike once a year and oil the brake and three- or five-speed hubs every six months with a lightweight machine oil. Some coaster brakes do not have an oil cup; this type has to be taken apart to lubricate. Five- and ten-speed derailleur type hubs have to be taken apart in order to grease the bearings. The sprocket cluster should be oiled every three months with a lightweight machine oil. The derailleur wheels should also be oiled every three months with a lightweight machine oil.

CLEANING THE BICYCLE

All bicycles are painted with either enamel or lacquer. Any type of auto wax applied to the bicycle when it is new will preserve the finish. On an old bicycle, use a wiper rag with a little kerosene and most of the dirt will come off. When the dirt is incrusted, a piece of light-grade steel wool will take it off with light rubbing. If too much pressure is applied, the painted surface will be scratched. After cleaning the bicycle, spray it with a coat of clear lacquer. This will bring back the gloss and preserve the finish at the same time.

The best and easiest method of cleaning chrome is with a Brillo pad, or just plain steel wool. As chrome is harder than steel wool, it will not scratch. When chrome has begun to rust, first remove the rust with the steel wool, then wipe it clean with

a rag, and spray the chrome with clear lacquer. This will prevent
it from rusting again.

TIRE PRESSURES AND REPAIR

The proper air pressure in a tire depends on the size of the
tire and also on the weight of the person riding the bicycle. The
following chart may be used to determine the proper air pressure. For people over 180 lbs., add 5 lbs. pressure to the tires.

16 x 1⅜ tires — 40 lbs. pressure
16 x 1.75   ” — 30   ”   ”
16 x 2.00   ” — 30   ”   ”
20 x 1⅜   ” — 40   ”   ”
20 x 1.75   ” — 35   ”   ”
20 x 2.125 ” — 35   ”   ”
24 x 1⅜   ” — 45   ”   ”
24 x 1.75   ” — 35   ”   ”
24 x 2.125 ” — 35   ”   ”
26 x 1⅜   ” — 50   ”   ”
26 x 1.75   ” — 35   ”   ”
26 x 2.125 ” — 35   ”   ”
27 x 1¼   ” — 60   ”   ”
27 x 1⅛   ” — 90   ”   ”

For track racing on the 27 x 1⅛ tires, 100 to 110 lbs. pressure is correct. For road racing on 27 x 1⅛ tires, 90 lbs. pressure
is recommended.

REPAIRING TIRES

There are two types of tires used on bicycles. Approximately
99 percent of all bicycles have inner tube tires. The other one
percent have "cement-on" or as they are sometimes called,
"sew-up" tires. The inner tube tires are held onto the rim of the
wheel by a steel edge on the tire. When the steel edge is broken,
the tire will not stay on the rim when inflated. At present, there
is no satisfactory method of repairing an inner tube tire that is
cut or broken at the edge or at any other part of the tire. The
inner tube itself can be patched.

There are several ways to find a hole in the inner tube. I shall
start with the easiest way and continue through the most difficult.
When the tire goes flat, always get off the bicycle immediately.

If you have the necessary tools at hand (patch kit, tire irons, and pump) chances are that you will be able to patch it in a few minutes. First, turn your bicycle upside down. Rotate the wheel slowly to see if you can find the cause of the flat tire, such as a tack, piece of glass, or a thorn. If one of these items is in the tire, before removing it, loosen the tire from the wheel (opposite the chain side of the bicycle if on the rear) without taking the wheel off the bicycle. The hole in the tube will be very close to where the tire was punctured. If you cannot see it immediately, then stretch the tube with your fingers near where it should be. If you still cannot find it, remove the tube from the tire and wheel. Inflate the tube as much as you can without causing the tube to bulge out at any spot. Then, keeping in mind where the puncture occurred on the tire, wet your lips and holding your face close to the inner tube, try to feel the air on your lips as it escapes from the tube. When you find the hole, patch it. If it is so tiny that it is almost impossible to see, you can put a scratch mark with a sharp object across the hole, or you may insert a pencil or pen point into the hole to make it larger. Then patch it and remove the object that caused the flat, and replace the tube in the tire and inflate.

If after using this method you still cannot find the hole, remove the wheel from the bicycle and inflate the tube as hard as you can without causing it to bulge out. Then test the tube by submerging it in water. If it bubbles at any point, you have found the leak. Never apply a patch on a wet surface. Dry the tube well and, after marking it, rough up the spot where the hole is. Apply a light coat of rubber cement, covering an area about 1½ times the size of the patch. Apply the patch when the cement is still a little tacky.

If the leak still has not been found, try moving the valve stem in several directions, while holding the tube under water, to see if the valve bubbles. Ninety-nine times out of 100, one of these methods of finding a leak will work. If the tire still deflates, it will go down very slowly, in 24 hours or more. Check the valve core when the tire is inflated by applying a little spit to the valve where the core is seated. If a small bubble forms, replace the valve core. If there is no bubble and the tire still deflates, you may repair it with a tire sealant which you put in through the valve stem after removing the valve core.

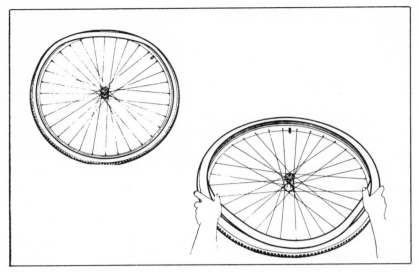

Fig. 12.   After outer cover is fully fitted, make sure that inner tube is not trapped anywhere between cover and rim by easing cover from edge of rim and examining both sides visually around the circumference. Relieve any traps by easing cover away from tube.

INSTALLING TIRES

When putting a new tube or tire onto a wheel, it is best to use tire irons rather than screw drivers so that there will be less chance of puncturing the tube. First put the valve stem of the tube through the hole of the rim. Then put one side of the tire on and inflate the tube just enough so that it will take its shape. Then, starting at the valve stem, force the rest of the tire on using your hands as much as possible rather than tools. When you have to use tire irons, be very careful not to pinch the tube as you force the tire onto the wheel.

CEMENT-ON TIRES

Cement-on, or sew-up tires are very difficult to repair. The tire has a tube but it is completely sealed with the casing on the outside, and a rubber liner cemented to the underside of the tire. In order to get to the tube, it is necessary to break the inner liner loose. This can be done with a razor blade. Then you must cut open the stitching that holds the casing together. After patching the tube, you must sew the casing together again and cement on the liner to cover the stitching.

Although this type of tire can be used without cementing the tire to the rim, it is better to cement on the tire as there is a possibility that the tire will move on the rim if it is not cemented. If the tire moves on the rim, it causes the valve stem to tear from the tire.

GENERAL CARE

The most important thing that the bicycle owner should do to keep his bicycle in good condition is to make sure that all nuts and bolts are tight. A loose nut or bolt can cause much damage. Although everything on a new bike should be in good order, there are many times when something is accidentally left loose; therefore check all nuts, bolts, and screws on the bicycle, making sure that they are tight, and you will save yourself a lot of work later. A periodic check (about once a month) is sufficient.

CHAIN ADJUSTMENT

On all bicycles that do not use a derailleur, the chain should be adjusted so that there is not more than ½″ slack when moved up and down at the center between the front and rear sprockets. On a derailleur-type bicycle, there is much more slack, and the adjustment is made in the derailleur itself. This will be explained in the chapter called "Derailleurs."

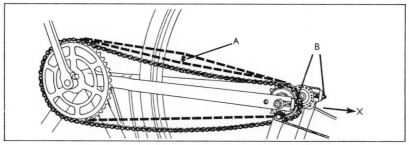

Fig. 13.   "A" shows proper chain adjustment.

CHAIN REPAIRING

All bicycle chains are made up of roller and connecting links. The roller link is the inner link and the connecting link is the outer link. When it is necessary to replace a broken outer link, all you would need is a master link. If the inner link is broken, you replace it with a roller link. All chain links are connected with chain rivets. To remove the rivet you must use a chain tool which forces the rivet out. If you do not have a chain tool you can use a center punch to start the rivet on its way and a nail to force it the rest of the way. Always try to force the rivet almost, but not quite all the way out. Allow the end of the rivet to remain a little inside the outer link so that it will be easy to put back if needed.

If on a ten-speed bicycle, there is one link that is so tight that is does not straighten out when the bicycle is ridden, it will cause the chain to slip when pedaling. To loosen a tight link, bend the chain back and forth at the place where the link is tight. This will free it.

Chapter III

Braking Systems

HAND BRAKES

Your bicycle will be fitted with either centerpull or sidepull brakes. Both types of brakes are highly efficient when correctly adjusted.

BRAKE ADJUSTMENT

The correct adjustment of your brakes exists when a minimum of movement of the brake lever brings the brake blocks into contact with the rim. The brake should not be so closely adjusted that the brake blocks touch the rim while in the "off" position.

CENTERPULL BRAKES

Centerpull brakes are actuated by means of a brake cable connected on one end to the brake handle, which is mounted on the handlebar, and at the other end to a bridging cable. The bridging cable is connected to both sides of the brake carriage. As the brake handle is squeezed, the brake shoes are pressed against the rim of the bicycle causing it to lock. The centerpull fine adjustment is made by the following procedure:

1. Loosen lock nut A.
2. Turn adjustor B to set blocks just clear of the rim.
3. Tighten lock nut A.

4. If one brake block is closer to the rim than the other, loosen the center bolt nut C and center the entire brake body. Then retighten center bolt nut C.

5. Tighten nuts D so that the brake blocks meet the rim squarely.

Adjustments on the centerpull brake can be made by taking up on the adjusting barrel which is located just below the handlebar stem. You may also take up slack in the cable by tightening the cable where it is fastened to the bridge that holds the bridging cable. Worn brake blocks and frayed cables should be replaced immediately.

SIDEPULL BRAKES

The sidepull brake is operated in the same manner as the centerpull brake. It differs from the centerpull brake in that the brake cable is attached to one side of the brake carriage instead of the center. It will operate evenly if you make sure that the spring on the brake carriage is centered evenly. If the brake shoes do not close evenly, you may center the brake by tapping the brake spring lightly with a hammer until the brake shoes center themselves. The brake may be adjusted by taking up on the adjusting screw fastened to the brake carriage, or by

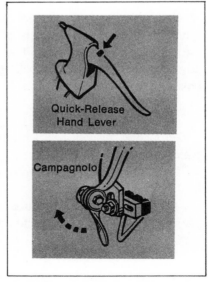

Fig. 14.   Side pull brake.   Fig. 15.   Quick-release mechanism.

tightening the brake cable at the eye bolt at the end of the cable. The sidepull brake fine adjustment is made by the following procedure:

1. Loosen lock nut A.
2. Turn adjustor B to set blocks just clear of the rim.
3. Tighten lock nut A.
4. If one brake block is closer to the rim than the other, adjust by tapping C on the opposite side. For Weinman brakes, loosen rear nut and re-center.
5. Tighten nuts D so that the brake blocks meet the rim squarely.

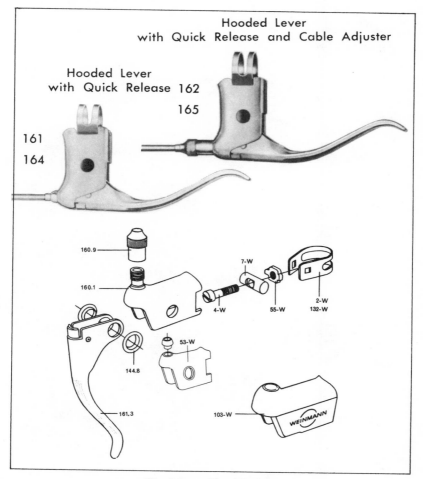

Fig. 16.   Hand levers.

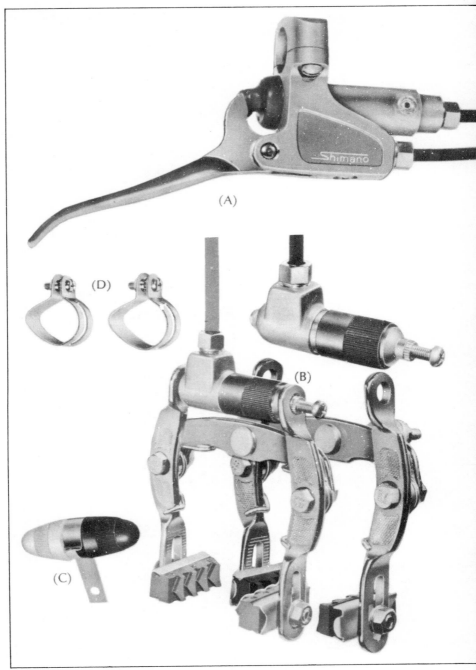

Fig. 17.   Oil pressure braking system.

An ordinary caliper-type rim brake applies braking power
the rim by pushing the brake shoe (rim friction rubber)
via a wire or rod.
This power brake is a completely new type which applies
grabbing power by using oil pressure from a master
cylinder through fluid lines to front and rear wheel cylinders

FEATURES

*Front and rear wheel brake controls are operated with one hand.
*Braking is done by two independent systems, the rear
  wheel brakes first when the brake lever is squeezed, then
  the front wheel. This is the ideal system.
*This system is especially outstanding for its extra safety.
  Even if one of the oil pressure tube should be broken,
  there is no danger, the master cyilnder contains independent
  oil pressure chambers for front and rear braking.
  At such a time the undamaged hose will provide strong,
  safe braking power.
*This power brake has no more wire problems, such as wire
  slack, rust, cutting, etc., which were always problems in
  ordinary brakes. This feature means added safety.
*The brake lever stroke can be freely adjusted in accordance
  with your desire.

COMPONENTS
Lever: 1 piece. (A)
Caliper brake: 1 piece, each. (B)
Oil reservoir: 1 piece. (C)
Cable clip band (1"): 2 pieces. (D)

QUICK-RELEASE BRAKE MECHANISM

Some brake levers are fitted with quick-release units. The
quick release allows you to open the brake stirrups further than
normal. By doing this, removal and fitting of the wheels is made
easier since the tire will be allowed to pass through the brake
blocks without deflating.

To operate the quick release, gently apply pressure to the
brake lever and press the quick-release button or knob with
your thumb. Then, holding the button or knob, allow the brake
lever to return past its normal position

The quick-release hand lever unit automatically resets itself
as soon as you use your brake.

Campagnolo brakes are fitted with a different type quick-release lever. A lever is located on the side of the brake stirrup. When the lever is down, the brake is set. To use your quick-release unit, it is necessary to pull the lever up. *Important*— Before riding, make sure that the lever is pushed down; otherwise your brake will not operate.

COASTER BRAKES

BENDIX

Although there are several different models of Bendix coaster brakes, they all operate in the same manner. As the brake is applied by putting pressure on the pedals in reverse (back pedaling), the driving screw (BB-502) causes the driving clutch (BB-159) to push toward the brake arm (BB-510) side of the hub. This motion in turn causes the brake shoes (BB-22) to expand against the hub shell, which causes the wheel to lock. The purpose of the brake arm is to prevent the stationary (BB-533) cone from turning as the brake is applied.

SERVICE INSTRUCTION FOR BENDIX COASTER BRAKE

A. Slippage occurs when bicycle is pedaled forward.
   Check for excessive wear on driving clutch, part BB-159. If small end of driving clutch extends $\frac{1}{16}''$ beyond the tapered shoulder in the hub, replace it.
B. Pedals rotate backwards excessively when brake is applied.
   Check for dirt wedged in driving clutch or driving end expander, part BB-159.
   Check all bearings to make sure they are not broken.
   Check adjustment of adjusting cone, part BB-7.
C. Poor braking.
   Check for wear on brake shoe, part BB-22. If worn, replace.
D. Brake fails to release after applying.
   Check for excessive dirt inside hub and make sure cones are adjusted so that wheel spins freely.
E. Cracking or grinding noise.
   Check for bent axle.
   Check for chain being too tight.

Check for proper cone adjustment.

Check for bent dust cap, part BB-558.

F. Squealing noise when brake is applied.

Check for worn brake shoes, part BB-22. If worn, replace.

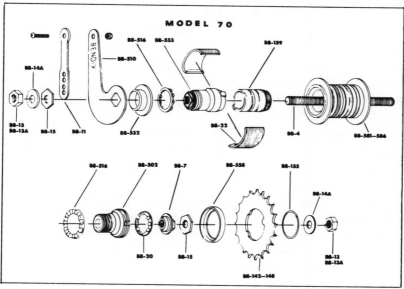

Fig. 18.   Exploded view of Bendix coaster brake.

SERVICING THE BENDIX COASTER BRAKE

When it is necessary to take the brake apart, always take it apart on the sprocket side. Remove the adjusting cone lock nut and the adjusting cone. Always make sure that the bearings are greased before reassembling. After the brake is assembled, make sure that the brake arm lock nut is tight against the brake arm before setting the adjustment on the adjusting cone. When the brake is properly adjusted, the wheel will spin freely and there will be no side play in the wheel. When reinstalling the wheel, make sure that the brake arm is fastened securely to the frame with a brake band. Lock the wheel in place in the center of the bicycle frame by tightening the axle nuts. Test the brake by turning the crank and applying back pressure to see that the brake holds.

BENDIX TWO-SPEED AUTOMATIC AND TWO-SPEED OVERDRIVE

The Bendix two-speed automatic and the two-speed overdrive change gears without any cables or hand controls. The driving gear ratio can be changed any time the rider desires by moving the pedals slightly in the braking direction.

The two-speed automatic is a planet geared unit consisting of a low-speed driver, high-speed driver, and sun gear. When these drivers rotate around the sun gear, they rotate at different speeds. For direct drive, the high-speed driver engages the high-speed clutch with the hub shell. The hub overrides the slower turning low-speed driver and clutch. Sprocket and hub turn at the same speed for direct drive.

For low-gear drive, back pedal the high-speed driver to disengage the high-speed clutch from the hub shell. This is done through the operation of the indexing spring. The slower turning low-speed driver will then engage the low-speed clutch with the hub shell. In low gear, the hub shell turns 32 percent slower than the sprocket.

The two-speed overdrive automatic is essentially the same as the two-speed automatic. It differs in that the overdrive sprocket is attached to the low-speed driver instead of the high-speed driver.

For direct drive, the indexing spring disengages the high-speed clutch from the hub shell, permitting the low-speed clutch to engage the hub shell. The hub shell and sprocket turn at the same speed.

For overdrive, back pedal the low-speed driver to engage the high-speed clutch with the hub shell. The faster moving hub shell will override the low-speed driver. The hub shell will turn 47 percent faster than the sprocket.

TO DISASSEMBLE

Hub should be in low-gear drive (hub turns slower than the sprocket). *This is a must to prevent possible damage to the coupling (AB21).*

Place axle at brake arm side in a vise and remove the adjusting cone lock nut. Holding the adjusting cone in a stationary position, turn the sprocket clockwise by hand while the sun gear (AB7) is unscrewed. After the adjusting cone and sun gear disengage from the low-speed screw assembly (AB328), remove it from the axle. (On overdrive models, put hub in direct drive—hub shell and sprocket turn at same speed.) This must be done to prevent damage to the coupling (AB21). Hold the sprocket still while unscrewing the adjusting cone and sun gear (AB7). Remove small ball retainer (AB20) from the low-speed driving screw (AB328). Remove the driving screw assemblies by turning the sprocket counterclockwise and pulling up. (In overdrive models, hold both driving screws together while removing them from the brake to prevent spilling of loose bearings.) Remove large ball retainer from the hub shell. Lift hub shell from inner assembly, holding hand around bottom of hub shell to prevent the four brake shoes (AB322) from dropping. Remove the four brake shoes. Remove the high-speed clutch and expander assembly (AB23, AB21, AB303, AB306).

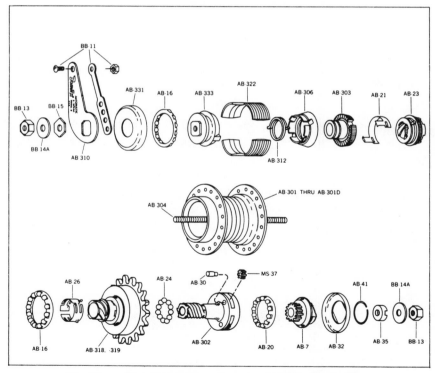

Fig. 19.   Bendix two-speed automatic with shoe brakes.

SUBASSEMBLIES MAY BE DISASSEMBLED AS FOLLOWS

The brake arm can be removed by unscrewing the lock nut next to it and prying off the brake arm.

The driver subassembly may be removed by lifting the low-speed driving screw (AB328) from the high-speed driving screw (AB318), being careful not to lose the loose bearings. The planet gear (MS37) can be removed by taking out the pins. (See Fig. 19.)

The clutch expander assembly comes apart by unhooking end of coupling (AB21) from slots of low-speed driving clutch (AB303). Unhook coupling from retarder spring on high-speed clutch. To separate low-speed driving clutch and drive end expander (AB306), pry up top side of retarder (AB312) with small screw driver and peel off.

Clean and dry all parts and replace worn or damaged parts. Grease brake parts except for the indexing spring and high-speed clutch, both of which should be oiled.

ASSEMBLY INSTRUCTIONS

Clutch and Expander Subassembly

Using low-speed driver for support only, screw on low-speed driving clutch drive-end expander with dentils facing each other. (See Fig. 21.) Remove assembly from low-speed driver.

Hook coupling on retarder spring of high-speed clutch. *Note: Low window of coupling should line up with low hook on spiral spring.* (See Fig. 22.)

Hook coupling into slots of low-speed driving clutch. (See Fig. 23.)

Drive Screw Assembly

Assemble indexing spring over sleeve of high-speed driving screw with the three short lugs against the shoulder of the ball race. (See Fig. 24.)

The planet gears are held in the low-speed driving screw by placing the pins flush with or below the surface of the screw. Place the eleven loose balls into the ball race of the high-speed driving screw. (The low-speed driver may be reversed and in-

Fig. 20.   Sun gear is threaded onto axle to engage planet gear in side of hub.

Fig. 21.   Driving clutch seated in expander with dentils (serrations) facing each other.

Fig. 22.   High-speed clutch hooks onto retarder spring.

Fig. 23.   Coupling hooked into slots of low-speed driving clutch.

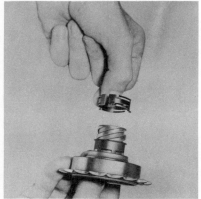

Fig. 24.   Three short lugs of indexing spring are placed over sleeve of high-speed driving screw.

serted and used as a guide while these balls are being placed.)
Assemble the drivers as shown in Fig. 25. Put a good coating of
grease on loose bearings and on internal gear of high-speed
driver. When assembling the brake arm, use the dust cap to
press the large ball retainer onto the anchor-end expander
(AB333). Screw anchor-end expander onto the axle, leaving
approximately 1⅛″ axle protruding. Install dust cap and brake
arm and tighten lock nut securely, as shown in Fig. 26.

Fig. 25.   Low-speed driver is fitted   Fig. 26.   Place dust cap on anchor
into high-speed driver.   and expander.

Hub Assembly

Insert high-speed clutch (AB23) and retarder assembly
(AB345) into hub as shown in Fig. 27. Insert shoe brakes in
hub shell around the driver-end expander (AB306) as shown in
Fig. 28. Insert brake arm assembly into hub shell and turn until
anchor-end expander (AB333) drops into place. (See Fig. 29.)

Invert assembly and clamp the arm side of axle in vise. Insert
large retainer (AB16) in hub shell with balls facing down.
Holding driving screws together, insert into hub, turning clockwise until seated (see Fig. 30). Insert small ball retainer (AB20)

Fig. 27.   High-speed clutch and retarder assembly are placed into hub.

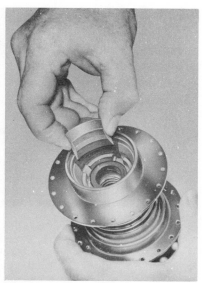

Fig. 28.   Shoe brakes are installed in hub around driver end expander.

Fig. 29.   Brake arm assembly is inserted into hub.

Fig. 30.   Driving screws are inserted into hub assembly.

into low-speed driver (AB328) with balls facing down. Turn adjusting cone and sun gear (AB7) on axle until sun gear touches the planet gears. Turn sun gear clockwise while turning the sprocket counterclockwise until sun gear is bottomed. Back sun gear off ⅛ turn and secure with lock nut. A trace of side play at the wheel rim should be noticed.

STURMEY ARCHER (PERRY) SC COASTER HUB

The Sturmey Archer Coaster Hub works on the principle of a driving clutch forcing a brass sleeve to expand. This causes the brake to stop the bicycle. To disassemble the coaster brake, remove the lock nut next to the brake arm (4). Unscrew the brake cone assembly (5), and lift wheel from coaster brake. If coaster brake does not have enough stopping power, replace brake band (13). If coaster brake clips forward, check drive rollers (22) for wear (replace if necessary). Check all bearings for wear. If worn or broken, replace. Lubricate all ball bearings with a light grade grease. Replace braking assembly by first fitting large ball retainer into hub shell. Place driver (23) on axle. Insert complete assembly into hub shell. Insert brake band (13) with flanges facing the brake arm side of hub shell. Screw on brake cone assembly (5) finger tight. Set brake arm in place. Screw on lock nut and lock tight against brake arm.

MAINTENANCE INSTRUCTION FOR THE STURMEY ARCHER SC COASTER HUB

The following simple instructions cover adjustment and lubrication of the coaster brake.

1. Loosen the two axle nuts (A).
2. Loosen the lock nut on the left-hand side of the wheel (B).
3. Using a crescent wrench on the square end of the axle (C), turn it clockwise to tighten the bearings or counterclockwise to loosen them.
4. Retighten the lock nut and axle nuts, leaving the wheel with just a trace of side play at the rim. Make sure that the brake arm clip is always tightened when replacing the wheel in the frame.

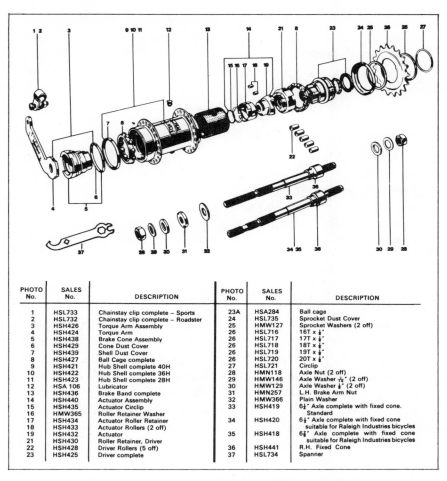

PHOTO No.	SALES No.	DESCRIPTION	PHOTO No.	SALES No.	DESCRIPTION
1	HSL733	Chainstay clip complete – Sports	23A	HSA284	Ball cage
2	HSL732	Chainstay clip complete – Roadster	24	HSL735	Sprocket Dust Cover
3	HSH426	Torque Arm Assembly	25	HMW127	Sprocket Washers (2 off)
4	HSH424	Torque Arm	26	HSL716	16T x ⅛″
5	HSH438	Brake Cone Assembly	26	HSL717	17T x ⅛″
6	HSH429	Cone Dust Cover	26	HSL718	18T x ⅛″
7	HSH439	Shell Dust Cover	26	HSL719	19T x ⅛″
8	HSH427	Ball Cage complete	26	HSL720	20T x ⅛″
9	HSH421	Hub Shell complete 40H	27	HSL721	Circlip
10	HSH422	Hub Shell complete 36H	28	HMN118	Axle Nut (2 off)
11	HSH423	Hub Shell complete 28H	29	HMW146	Axle Washer ₇⁄₁₆″ (2 off)
12	HSA 106	Lubricator	30	HMW129	Axle Washer ⅜″ (2 off)
13	HSH436	Brake Band complete	31	HMN257	L.H. Brake Arm Nut
14	HSH440	Actuator Assembly	32	HMW366	Plain Washer
15	HSH435	Actuator Circlip	33	HSH419	6¼″ Axle complete with fixed cone. Standard
16	HMW365	Roller Retainer Washer			
17	HSH434	Actuator Roller Retainer	34	HSH420	6¼″ Axle complete with fixed cone suitable for Raleigh Industries bicycles
18	HSH433	Actuator Rollers (2 off)			
19	HSH432	Actuator	35	HSH418	6⅞″ Axle complete with fixed cone suitable for Raleigh Industries bicycles
21	HSH430	Roller Retainer, Driver			
22	HSH428	Driver Rollers (5 off)	36	HSH441	R.H. Fixed Cone
23	HSH425	Driver complete	37	HSL734	Spanner

Fig. 31.   Sturmey Archer (Perry) SC coaster hub.

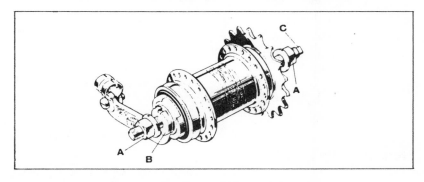

Fig. 32.   Sturmey Archer coaster brake.

Fasten brake arm clip through bicycle frame and brake arm. Tighten axle nuts with washers against frame. Check wheel for proper alignment (wheel must be in center of frame). Check hub brake for proper adjustment (wheel must spin freely and at the same time not have any side play). Test coaster brake by applying it and making sure that wheel locks.

STURMEY ARCHER THREE-SPEED COASTER BRAKE

The Sturmey Archer three-speed brake provides a normal gear, a low gear (25 percent lower than normal), and a high gear (33⅓ higher). The Sturmey Archer three-speed coaster brake, besides having three speeds, also has a coaster brake. When changing gears, the rider must pedal and then slack up on pedaling before changing.

TO DISASSEMBLE

Remove lock nut on brake arm side (26 and 27), lock washer (28), and adjusting nut (29). Lift off brake arm and cone assembly (4). Take out ball retainer (8) and brake band (10) from hub shell. Turn wheel over and remove right-hand wheel nut (42), wheel washer, and cone lock nut (41). Unscrew right-hand ball ring (20) (use hammer and punch). Withdraw gear from hub shell. Remove the brake thrust plate (12) and planet cage pawl ring (13). Unscrew cone (39). Lift off clutch spring cap (36), spring (35) driver assembly (21), ball ring (20), ratchet ring (19), gear ring for pawl ring (18), and gear ring 17). Unscrew gear indicator coupling (43), lift off clutch (34), and remove axle key (33). Take out planet pinion pins (15) and remove planet pinions (14). Push off circlip (30) from left end of axle and lift off planet cage.

POINTS TO CHECK

Check axle for straightness by rolling on table. Check all gear teeth for wear and chipping. Check all pawls and ratchets for wear (they must fit perfectly). Check all other parts for wear (see that there is no slack when fitting together). Check brake arm for fitting in its recess (there should not be any side play).

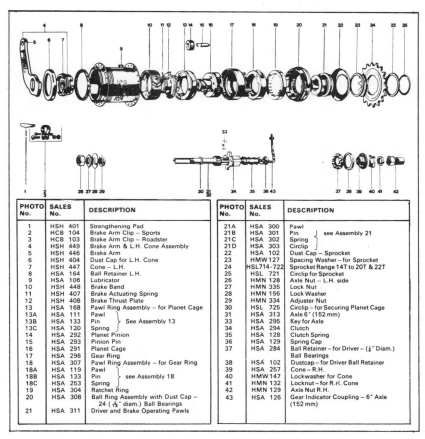

PHOTO No.	SALES No.	DESCRIPTION	PHOTO No.	SALES No.	DESCRIPTION
1	HSH 401	Strengthening Pad	21A	HSA 300	Pawl
2	HCB 104	Brake Arm Clip – Sports	21B	HSA 301	Pin ⎫ see Assembly 21
3	HCB 103	Brake Arm Clip – Roadster	21C	HSA 302	Spring ⎬
4	HSH 449	Brake Arm & L.H. Cone Assembly	21D	HSA 303	Circlip ⎭
5	HSH 446	Brake Arm	22	HSA 102	Dust Cap – Sprocket
6	HSH 404	Dust Cap for L.H. Cone	23	HMW 127	Spacing Washer – for Sprocket
7	HSH 447	Cone – L.H.	24	HSL714-722	Sprocket Range 14T to 20T & 22T
8	HSA 164	Ball Retainer L.H.	25	HSL 721	Circlip for Sprocket
9	HSA 106	Lubricator	26	HMN 128	Axle Nut – L.H. side
10	HSH 448	Brake Band	27	HMN 335	Lock Nut
11	HSH 407	Brake Actuating Spring	28	HMN 156	Lock Washer
12	HSH 408	Brake Thrust Plate	29	HMN 334	Adjuster Nut
13	HSA 168	Pawl Ring Assembly – for Planet Cage	30	HSL 725	Circlip – for Securing Planet Cage
13A	HSA 111	Pawl ⎫	31	HSA 313	Axle 6″ (152 mm)
13B	HSA 133	Pin ⎬ See Assembly 13	33	HSA 295	Key for Axle
13C	HSA 120	Spring ⎭	34	HSA 294	Clutch
14	HSA 292	Planet Pinion	35	HSA 128	Clutch Spring
15	HSA 293	Pinion Pin	36	HSA 129	Spring Cap
16	HSA 291	Planet Cage	37	HSA 284	Ball Retainer – for Driver – (¼″ Diam.)
17	HSA 296	Gear Ring			Ball Bearings
18	HSA 307	Pawl Ring Assembly – for Gear Ring	38	HSA 102	Dustcap – for Driver Ball Retainer
18A	HSA 119	Pawl ⎫	39	HSA 257	Cone – R.H.
18B	HSA 133	Pin ⎬ see Assembly 18	40	HMW 147	Lockwasher for Cone
18C	HSA 253	Spring ⎭	41	HMN 132	Locknut – for R.H. Cone
19	HSA 304	Ratchet Ring	42	HMN 129	Axle Nut R.H.
20	HSA 308	Ball Ring Assembly with Dust Cap – 24 (7/32″ diam.) Ball Bearings	43	HSA 126	Gear Indicator Coupling – 6″ Axle (152 mm)
21	HSA 311	Driver and Brake Operating Pawls			

Fig. 33.   Sturmey Archer three-speed coaster brake.

Fig. 34.   Sturmey Archer three-speed coaster brake.

TO ASSEMBLE

Fit together gear pawls, pins, and springs. Rivet the pawl pins securely in position. Assemble brake-operating pawls, springs, pins, and circlip in driver. Assemble sprocket dust cap, spacing washer, and sprocket in arrangement noted when dismantling the hub, and add circlip. Fit the ball retainer (37) into the driver (21) (the ring of retainer faces outward) and fit dust cap (38). (Use light grease on inner surface of dust cap.) Fit together planet cage pawls, pins, and springs. Rivet the pawl pins securely into position. Fit 24 ball bearings ($\frac{3}{16}$" diameter) into ball race of right-hand ball retainer (20). Grease bearings. Press in inner dust cap. Make sure the bearings revolve freely after dust cap has been fitted. Place dust cap (9) over left-hand cone (7), and press brake arm (5) tightly into cone slots. Grease ball track of the left-hand cone.

Place the right-hand end of the axle in a vise—the slot for the axle key is below the sun pinion—and fit in the planet cage (16) (actuator thread uppermost) and push circlip (30) into axle groove. Reverse axle in vise, add the planet pinions (14) and pins (15), making sure that the D-shape ends of the pins are facing downward. Fit axle key (33) into axle slot (with the hole of the key facing upwards), slide clutch (34) over axle and key, and screw gear indicator rod (43) into key. Fit on the gear ring (17) and the previously prepared gear-ring pawl ring. Insure that the heads of the pawl pins are facing upwards. Insert the ratchet ring (19) into the right-hand ball ring (20) and place these over the gear ring assembly (ratchet ring dogs must engage gear ring). Fit in the previously prepared driver. Slide the clutch spring (35) over the axle and fit on spring cap (36). Screw the right-hand cone (39) onto axle (finger tight), then slacken half a turn and lock in position with the washer (40) and lock nut (41). Do not unscrew cone more than $\frac{5}{8}$ths of a turn, as this would throw the gear mechanism out of adjustment. Now turn the assembled mechanism upside down in the vise. Place the planet cage pawl ring (Fig. 35) over the flats on the pinion pins. Fit in the brake thrust plate (12). The leg of the actuating spring must face outward, as in Fig. 35, and the thrust plate must engage fully the dogs on the planet cage pawl ring. Next, fit the brake band (10) over the brake thrust plate (12)

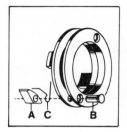
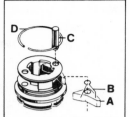
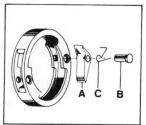

Fig. 35.
Thrust plate showing
pawl and spring.

Fig. 36.
Planet cage showing
position of pawl and
spring before insertion.

Fig. 37.
Pawl ring assembly.

so that the inner band projections face up. Now the mechanism
is completely assembled. With the wheel in a horizontal position,
place the assembly into the hub shell from below and screw in
the right-hand ball ring (20).

Tighten the ball ring with a punch and hammer. Fit the ball
retainer into the left-hand ball retainer with the balls facing
down. Fit together the left-hand cone and brake arm assembly
(4), making sure that the brake band projections and actuating
spring leg fit into their respective slots in the cone.

Screw the adjusting nut (29) on the axle, then the lock
washer and lock nut. Tighten lock nut against adjuster nut so
that the wheel will spin freely and not have any side play. Replace the wheel into the frame and tighten axle nuts. Fasten
brake clip to brake arm.

When adjusting the actuating chain, make sure that it is
threaded all the way into the axle and that the cable connecting
the actuating chain is fastened so that all the slack is removed
from it when it is in high gear.

When taking the slack out of the cable, make sure that you
do not get it too tight, as this will cause a bad adjustment.

The following Gear Correction Guide may be used if you
cannot get all three gears to operate correctly.

GEAR CORRECTION GUIDE

NOTE: The major cause of trouble is faulty gear adjustment.
Check to see that the end of the indicator rod is level with the
end of the right hand end of the axle when gear control lever

is in No. 2 gear position. If the complaint is sluggish gear change or stiffness, this may point to LACK OF OIL. Hub and control should be oiled and re-tested before going further. If the fault persists, the following chart should locate the trouble.

SYMPTOM	FAULT	REMEDY
No low gear (1st)	1. Low-gear pawls upside down or pointing in wrong direction.	1. Reassemble pawls correctly.
	2. Distorted axle spring.	2. Fit new axle spring.
Slipping in low gear (1st)	1. Sliding clutch, worn or chipped at corners.	1. Fit new sliding clutch.
	2. Indicator not screwed in fully in axle key.	2. Screw in indicator fully.
	3. R.H. cone wrongly adjusted.	3. Readjust R.H. cone.
	4. Kinks in gear control wire.	4. Fit new control cable.
	5. Gear indicator coupling twisted by over-tightening.	5. Replace or refit as required.
Fluctuating between low gear (1st) and normal gear (2nd)	1. Faulty or worn gear ring pawls.	1. Change both gear ring pawls.
Slipping in normal gear (2nd)	1. Gear ring dogs and/or sliding clutch chipped, due to incorrect gear adjustment or gear changing.	1. Fit new gear ring and/or sliding clutch.

SYMPTOM	FAULT	REMEDY
	2. Indicator not screwed in fully in axle key.	2. Screw in indicator fully.
Slipping in top gear (3rd)	1. Pinion pins or sliding clutch badly worn due to bad adjustment.	1. Fit new parts.
	2. Weak or distorted axle spring.	2. Fit new spring.
	3. Incorrect R.H. cone adjustment.	3. Readjust.
Hub runs stiffly. Drag on pedals when free wheeling.	1. Too many balls in ball ring.	1. 24 balls only should be fitted.
	2. Cones excessively tight.	2. Readjust cones.
	3. Chainstay ends not parallel.	3. Correct chainstay ends. It is essential that the ends are parallel, otherwise the axle will be strained when the nuts are tightened and gear internals may be seriously affected.
	4. Corrosion due to inferior oil or LACK OF LUBRICATION.	4. Clean hub thoroughly and oil. Use Sturmey-Archer oil – or SAE20.
	5. Distorted dust caps.	5. Check dust caps and replace damaged caps.
Sluggish gear change.	1. Distorted clutch spring.	1. Replace spring.
	2. Bent axle.	2. Replace axle.

SYMPTOM	FAULT	REMEDY
	3. Worn chain links in gear indicator coupling.	3. Replace indicator and chain.
	4. Cable guide pulley out of line.	4. Correct alignment of cable and pulley on cycle frame.
	5. Lack of lubrication of gear cable.	5. Lubricate, or replace cable.

STURMEY ARCHER THREE-SPEED HUB

TO DISMANTLE THE AW HUB

1. Remove left-hand lock nuts (1) and (3), washers (2) and (4), and cone (5).
2. Unscrew right-hand ball ring (25) from hub shell (9) (use hammer and punch) and withdraw gear unit.
3. Detach the low-gear pawls (15), pins (16) and springs (24). Take off the right-hand locknut (3), washers (32) and (2), and cone (5).
4. Lift off clutch spring cap (40), and spring (39), driver (27), ball ring (25), and gear ring (22).
5. Detach gear-ring pawls (23), pins (16), and springs (24).
6. Remove thrust ring (37), unscrew indicator rod (36).
7. Push out axle key (34), take off sliding clutch (21), and sleeve (20).
8. Lift off planet cage (17), remove pinions (18) and pins (19).

POINTS TO CHECK

1. Freedom of clutch in driver. This should slide up and down easily.
2. Axle between centers for straightness.
3. All gear teeth for wear or chipping.
4. All races for wear (six in all).
5. Pinion pins, sliding clutch, and gear ring dogs for rounding off on engagement points.
6. Pawls and pawl ratchets for wear.

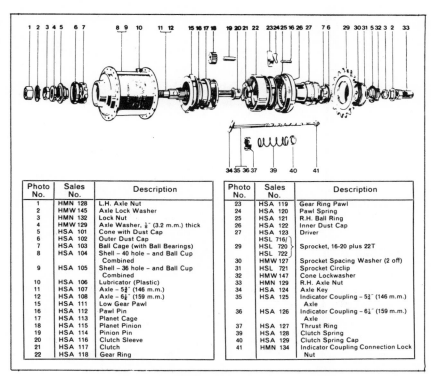

Photo No.	Sales No.	Description	Photo No.	Sales No.	Description
1	HMN 128	L.H. Axle Nut	23	HSA 119	Gear Ring Pawl
2	HMW 145	Axle Lock Washer	24	HSA 120	Pawl Spring
3	HMN 132	Lock Nut	25	HSA 121	R.H. Ball Ring
4	HMW 129	Axle Washer, ⅛″ (3.2 m.m.) thick	26	HSA 122	Inner Dust Cap
5	HSA 101	Cone with Dust Cap	27	HSA 123	Driver
6	HSA 102	Outer Dust Cap		HSL 716	
7	HSA 103	Ball Cage (with Ball Bearings)	29	HSL 720	Sprocket, 16-20 plus 22T
8	HSA 104	Shell – 40 hole – and Ball Cup Combined		HSL 722	
9	HSA 105	Shell – 36 hole – and Ball Cup Combined	30	HMW 127	Sprocket Spacing Washer (2 off)
			31	HSL 721	Sprocket Circlip
10	HSA 106	Lubricator (Plastic)	32	HMW 147	Cone Lockwasher
11	HSA 107	Axle – 5¾″ (146 m.m.)	33	HMN 129	R.H. Axle Nut
12	HSA 108	Axle – 6¼″ (159 m.m.)	34	HSA 124	Axle Key
15	HSA 111	Low Gear Pawl	35	HSA 125	Indicator Coupling – 5¾″ (146 m.m.) Axle
16	HSA 112	Pawl Pin			
17	HSA 113	Planet Cage	36	HSA 126	Indicator Coupling – 6¼″ (159 m.m.) Axle
18	HSA 115	Planet Pinion			
19	HSA 114	Pinion Pin	37	HSA 127	Thrust Ring
20	HSA 116	Clutch Sleeve	39	HSA 128	Clutch Spring
21	HSA 117	Clutch	40	HSA 129	Clutch Spring Cap
22	HSA 118	Gear Ring	41	HMN 134	Indicator Coupling Connection Lock Nut

Fig. 38.   Sturmey Archer three-speed hub.

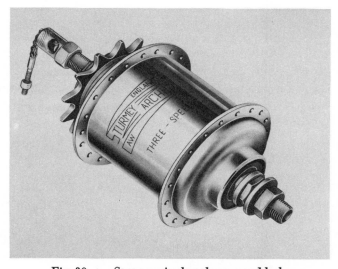

Fig. 39.   Sturmey Archer three-speed hub.

TO ASSEMBLE THE AW HUB

1. Hold axle (11) in a vise (slot for axle key above the sun pinion) and fit on the planet cage (17).
2. Add the planet pinions and pins (18) and (19).
3. Fit on sleeve (20), clutch (21), axle key (34), and screw in the indicator rod (36).
4. Locate thrust ring (37) over axle key (34).
5. Place pawls (23), pins (16), and springs (24) into gear ring (22). See Fig. 40, and fit this over planet cage (17).
6. Position the right-hand ball ring (25) over gear ring (22).
7. Add the driver (27), complete with fittings. (See Fig. 41.)
8. Slide clutch spring (39) and cap (40) over the axle.
9. Screw the right-hand cone (5) finger tight. Then slacken it a half turn and lock in that position with lock washer (32) and lock nut (3). *Note:* Cone must not be unscrewed more than half a turn as this would throw the gear mechanism out of adjustment.
10. Fit the planet cage pawl (15), pins and springs (23) and (24). (See Fig. 42.)
11. Screw the gear unit into the hub shell and tighten ball ring (25).
12. Screw on left-hand cone (5), add washers (4) and (2) and lock nut (3), and adjust the hub bearings.

GEAR ADJUSTMENT (See Fig. 43).

Place the gear control in No. 2 position. Screw the cable connection (3) until the end of the indicator rod is exactly level with the extreme end of the axle. This can be seen through the "window" in the right-hand nut (1). Now tighten locknut (2). *All Gears Are Now Set.*

GEAR ADJUSTMENT

Right side cone adjustment. Screw cone down finger tight, then slacken half a turn and lock in this position. *Note:* Turning it back more than this will affect the gear engagement.

On the left side, loosen lock nut and adjust the cone suitably; then retighten lock nut. A correctly adjusted wheel has a trace of side play at the rim.

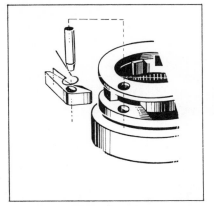

Fig. 40.   Pawl, pin, and spring all fit into gear ring.

Fig. 41.   Driver and fittings.

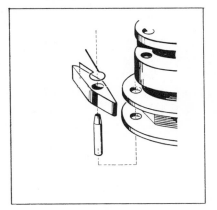

Fig. 42.   Pawl, pin, and spring all fit into planet cage.

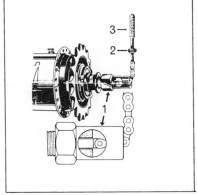

Fig. 43.   Three-speed hub showing gear adjustment.

GEAR CORRECTION GUIDE (AW GEAR)

Note: The major cause of trouble is faulty gear adjustment. Check to see that the end of the indicator rod is level with end of axle when gear control is in No. 2 position. If the complaint is sluggish gear change or stiffness, this may point to lack of oil.

SYMPTOM	FAULT	REMEDY
Slipping in low gear (1st)	1. Sliding clutch worn	1. Replace

SYMPTOM	FAULT	REMEDY
	2. Indicator not screwed in fully	2. Readjust
	3. R.H. cone incorrectly adjusted	3. Readjust
	4. Kinks in control wire	4. Replace
	5. Twisted indicator chain	5. Replace
Self-changing gear action between 1st gear and 2nd gear	1. Worn gear ring pawls	1. Replace
Slipping in normal gear (2nd)	1. Gear ring dogs and/or clutch worn	1. Replace
Slipping in top gear (3rd)	1. Pinion pins and/or clutch worn	1. Replace
	2. Weak or distorted axle spring	2. Fit new spring
	3. Incorrect R.H. cone adjustment	3. Readjust
	4. Grit between clutch sleeve and axle	4. Clean
Hub runs stiffly Drag on pedals	1. Too many balls in ballring	1. Fit in 24 only
	2. Cones too tight	2. Readjust
	3. Chainstay ends not parallel	3. Correct
	4. Corrosion	4. Clean and use S.A. oil
	5. Distorted dust caps	5. Replace
Sluggish gear change	1. Distorted axle spring	1. Replace
	2. Bent axle	2. Replace
	3. Worn indicator chain link	3. Replace
	4. Lack of oil, or frayed wire	4. Oil or replace

STURMEY ARCHER FIVE-SPEED HUB GEAR

TO DISMANTLE THE S5 HUB

1. Remove from left-hand side: bell crank (1), axle nut (2), lock washer (3), lock nut (4), washer (5), and cone (6).
2. Unscrew right-hand ball ring (21) from hub shell (9) (using hammer and punch) and withdraw internals.
3. Hold axle in a vise; remove right-hand axle nut (29), washer (3), lock nut (4), cone lock washer (28), and cone (6).
4. Lift off clutch spring (47) and cap (48), driver assembly (23), ball ring (21), and gear ring (18).
5. Remove thrusting ring (45). Push out axle key (44) and remove the clutch sleeve (42) and sliding clutch (43).
6. Push out pinion pins (17) and remove the pinions (16) and planet cage (12). The low gear pawl pins are riveted in position (if necessary to remove them, file riveted part flat.)
7. To remove sun pinions: Unscrew locknut (32), lock washer (33) and dog ring (34).
8. Push sun pinions (37) and (38) on to the axle dogs and pull out sleeve (36) from under the smaller one. Push out axle key (35).
9. Slide sun pinions, sleeve and low-gear spring (39) off the axle.

POINTS TO CHECK

1. Slide clutch up and down inside driver, to see that movement is free.
2. Make sure only 24 balls (3/16 inch diameter) are in right-hand ball ring.
3. Examine gear ring for cracks, chipping, or signs of wear on internal dogs and teeth.
4. Check that axle is straight.

EXAMINE FOR WEAR ON ENGAGAGEMENT POINTS

5. All ball races.
6. Sliding clutch.
7. All pinion teeth.
8. Planet cage dogs and gear ring dogs.
9. All pawls and pawl ratchets.
10. Axle dogs.

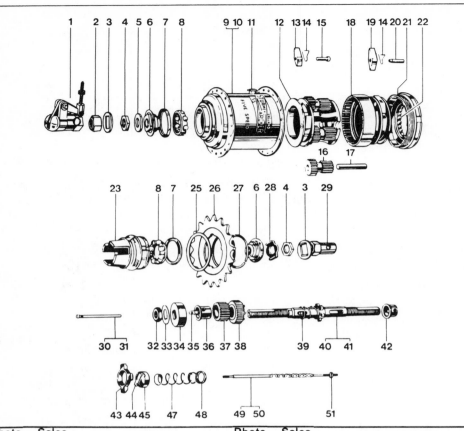

Photo No.	Sales No.	Description	Photo No.	Sales No.	Description
1	HSJ 679	Bellcrank (Steel)	28	HMW 147	Cone Lockwasher
2	HMN 128	Left-hand Axle Nut	29	HMN 129	Right-hand Axle Nut
3	HMW 145	Axle Washer	30	HSA 287	Gear Push Rod 6″ Axle (152 mm)
4	HMN 132	Locknut	31	HSA 288	Gear Push Rod 6¼″ Axle (159 mm)
5	HMW 129	Axle Spacing Washer ⅛″ (3.2 m.m.)	32	HMN 133	Locknut for Dog-Ring
6	HSA 101	Cone	33	HMW 149	Lockwasher for Dog-Ring
7	HSA 102	Outer Dust Cap	34	HSA 138	Dog-Ring
8	HSA 103	Ball Cage	35	HSA 268	Low Gear Axle Key
9	HSA 271	Shell – 40 hole – and Ball Cup Combined	36	HSA 140	Pinion Sleeve
10	HSA 270	Shell – 36 hole – and Ball Cup Combined	37	HSA 141	Secondary Sun Pinion
11	HSA 106	Lubricator (Plastic)	38	HSA 269	Primary Sun Pinion
12	HSA 132	Planet Cage	39	HSA 273	Low Gear Spring
13	HSA 111	Low Gear Pawl	40	HSA 274	Axle – 6″ (152 mm)
14	HSA 120	Pawl Spring	41	HSA 145	Axle – 6¼″ (159 mm)
15	HSA 133	Pawl Pin – Planet Cage	42	HSA 116	Clutch Sleeve
16	HSA 134	Planet Pinion	43	HSA 117	Clutch
17	HSA 135	Pinion Pin	44	HSA 124	Axle Key
18	HSA 118	Gear Ring	45	HSA 127	Thrust Ring
19	HSA 119	Gear Ring Pawl	47	HSA 128	Clutch Spring
20	HSA 112	Pawl Pin – Gear Ring	48	HSA 129	Spring Cap
21	HSA 121	Right-hand Ball Ring	49	HSA 126	Gear Indicator Rod Right-hand 6″ Axle (152 mm)
22	HSA 122	Inner Dust Cap			
23	HSA 123	Driver	50	HSA 126	Gear Indicator Rod Right-hand 6¼″ Axle (159 mm)
25	HMW 127	Sprocket Spacing Washer			
26	HSL 716–720	Sprocket – 16-20T	51	HMN 134	Connector Locknut
27	HSL 721	Sprocket Circlip			

Fig. 44.   Sturmey Archer five-speed hub gear.

TO REASSEMBLE THE S5 HUB

1. Prepare subassemblies. See Figs. 45, 46, and 47.
   - (a) Fit the pawls, pins, and springs into the gear ring. (See Fig. 45.)
   - (b) Assemble driver sprocket, spacing washers, circlip. (See Fig. 46.)
   - (c) Rivet the pawls, pins, and springs into the planet cage. (See Fig. 47.)

2. From the left (short slot) end of the axle, slide on low gear spring (39), primary sun pinion (38), secondary sun pinion (37), and sleeve (36), in that order.

3. Hold pinions up to the axle dogs—withdraw the sleeve until keyhole is exposed; insert key (35).
   Note: The hole through the key must be in line with the bore of axle. Release the pinions and secure the key.

4. Fit the dog ring (34) over axle "square," and secondary sun pinion teeth; secure with lock washer (33), and lock nut (32) (turn down edge of lock washer over two sides of lock nut).

5. From the right: Fit in the planet cage assembly (12).

6. Add planet pinions (16) and (17). The marked teeth must point radially outwards as in Fig. 48. To check the "timing," engage the gear ring with the pinions. It should rotate quite freely. Remove gear ring.

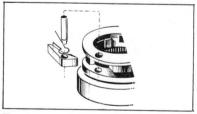

Fig. 45.   Pawl, pin, and spring all fit into planet gear.

Fig. 46.   Driver sprocket assembly.

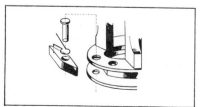

Fig. 47.   Pawl, pin, and spring all fit into planet cage.

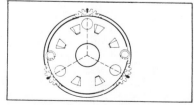

Fig. 48.   Marked teeth on planet pinions.

7. Fit on clutch sleeve (42) (flange first), the sliding clutch (43) (with the recess over the flange of the sleeve), the key (44), and the thrust ring (45).

8. Push indicator rod (49) into right end of axle and screw into axle key (44).

9. Fit on gear ring assembly (18), the right-hand ball ring (21), the driver assembly (23), the clutch spring (47), and cap (48).

10. Screw on right-hand cone (6) (finger tight). Then slacken it half a turn and lock in that position with lock washer (28) and lock nut (4). *Do not* unscrew more than half a turn.

11. Oil gear, and screw mechanism into hub shell (9) and tighten ball ring (21).

12. Fit in left-hand cone, (6), washer (5), and lock nut (4), and adjust the hub bearing.

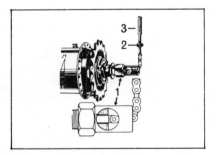

Fig. 49.   Adjustments on right side of hub gear.

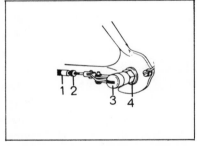

Fig. 50.   Adjustment on left side of axle.

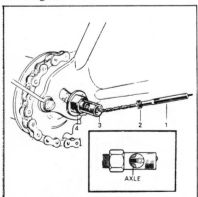

Fig. 51.   Right side adjustment of five-speed hub.

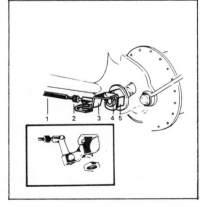

Fig. 52.   Left side adjustment of five-speed hub.

ADJUST HUB GEAR AS FOLLOWS:

1. With the right-hand control lever in central position, screw down lock nut (2).
2. Look through the circular "window" in the chain guide (Fig. 51) and screw down cable adjuster (1) until you see that the last link in the chain is clear of the axle.
3. Now adjust cable until *the end of rod is exactly level with the outside end of the axle* as shown in Fig. 51.
4. Now tighten lock nut (2) to cable adjuster (1).

LEFT-HAND SIDE (FIGURE 52)

First remove bellcrank and lock nut (Fig. 52) from rear frame tube and fit bellcrank (3) to left-hand axle nut (5) and lock it in position on axle with lock nut (4).

1. Now screw down lock nut (2).
2. Push left-hand lever to forward position, and screw cable connector to bellcrank a few turns only.
3. Push level to backward position and screw cable until all slackness in cable is taken up.
4. Applying light pressure, push the bellcrank arm forward and at the same time turn the wheel backward or forward. If gears are not fully engaged the bellcrank arm will move further forward.

STURMEY ARCHER THREE-SPEED HUB WITH EXPANDER BRAKE

TO DISMANTLE HUB

1. Remove axle nuts (9) and (51) and lock washers (10).
2. Remove left-hand lock nut (8), washer (11), notched adjusting washer (7), and spacing washer (20).
3. Lift off the brake unit—care should be taken not to lose the inner spacing washers (18) and (20), on the left-hand cone.
4. Unscrew left-hand cone (22).
5. Unscrew right-hand ball ring (41) (use hammer and punch) from shell (24/25) and withdraw gear unit.
6. Remove the low-gear pawls (32), pins (31), and springs (33) from the planet cage.
7. Place the left-hand end of the axle in a vise and remove the right-hand cone lock nut (8), washers if any, cone lock washer (50), and cone (45).

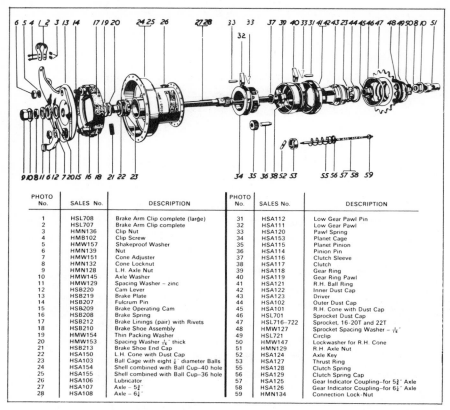

PHOTO No.	SALES No.	DESCRIPTION	PHOTO No.	SALES No.	DESCRIPTION
1	HSL708	Brake Arm Clip complete (large)	31	HSA112	Low Gear Pawl Pin
2	HSL707	Brake Arm Clip complete	32	HSA111	Low Gear Pawl
3	HMN136	Clip Nut	33	HSA120	Pawl Spring
4	HMB102	Clip Screw	34	HSA153	Planet Cage
5	HMW157	Shakeproof Washer	35	HSA115	Planet Pinion
6	HMN139	Nut	36	HSA114	Pinion Pin
7	HMW151	Cone Adjuster	37	HSA116	Clutch Sleeve
8	HMN132	Cone Locknut	38	HSA117	Clutch
9	HMN128	L.H. Axle Nut	39	HSA118	Gear Ring
10	HMW145	Axle Washer	40	HSA119	Gear Ring Pawl
11	HMW129	Spacing Washer – zinc	41	HSA121	R.H. Ball Ring
12	HSB220	Cam Lever	42	HSA122	Inner Dust Cap
13	HSB219	Brake Plate	43	HSA123	Driver
14	HSB207	Fulcrum Pin	44	HSA102	Outer Dust Cap
15	HSB209	Brake Operating Cam	45	HSA101	R.H. Cone with Dust Cap
16	HSB208	Brake Spring	46	HSL701	Sprocket Dust Cap
17	HSB212	Brake Linings (pair) with Rivets	47	HSL716–722	Sprocket, 16-20T and 22T
18	HSB210	Brake Shoe Assembly	48	HMW127	Sprocket Spacing Washer – $\frac{1}{16}$"
19	HMW154	Thin Packing Washer	49	HSL721	Circlip
20	HMW153	Spacing Washer $\frac{1}{16}$" thick	50	HMW147	Lockwasher for R.H. Cone
21	HSB213	Brake Shoe End Cap	51	HMN129	R.H. Axle Nut
22	HSA150	L.H. Cone with Dust Cap	52	HSA124	Axle Key
23	HSA103	Ball Cage with eight $\frac{1}{4}$" diameter Balls	53	HSA127	Thrust Ring
24	HSA154	Shell combined with Ball Cup–40 hole	54	HSA128	Clutch Spring
25	HSA155	Shell combined with Ball Cup–36 hole	55	HSA129	Clutch Spring Cap
26	HSA106	Lubricator	56	HSA125	Gear Indicator Coupling–for $5\frac{3}{4}$" Axle
27	HSA107	Axle – $5\frac{3}{4}$"	57	HSA126	Gear Indicator Coupling–for $6\frac{1}{4}$" Axle
28	HSA108	Axle – $6\frac{1}{4}$"	58	HSA126	
			59	HMN134	Connection Lock-Nut

Fig. 53.   Sturmey Archer three-speed hub with expander brakes.

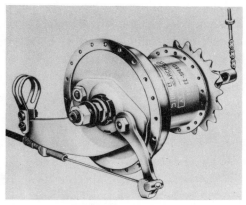

Fig. 54.   Sturmey Archer three-speed hub with expander brakes.

8. Lift off, in the following order, the clutch spring (55), cap (56), driver assembly (43), right-hand ball ring (41), and the gear ring (39).
9. Push out the gear-pawl pins (31), from the gear ring (39), to release the pawls (40) and springs (33).
10. Remove the thrust ring (53) and unscrew the indicator coupling (57) or (58).
11. Push out the axle key (52) and remove the sliding clutch (38) and sleeve (37).
12. Lift off the complete planet cage (34).
13. Take out the pinion pins (36) and remove the pinions (35) from the planet cage (34).
14. If it is necessary to remove the brake shoes (18) and linings (17) from the brake plate (13), unscrew the cam lever nut (6), and pull the cam lever (12) from the squared end of the cam. Then remove the nut (6), and shakeproof washer (5), securing the fulcrum pin (14), and lift off the brake shoes (18).

POINTS TO CHECK

Gear

1. Freedom of clutch in driver. This should slide up and down easily.
2. Axle between centers for straightness.
3. All gear teeth for wear or chipping.
4. All races for wear or pitting (six in all).
5. Pinion pins, clutch, and gear-ring dogs for rounding off on engagement points.
6. Pawls and pawl ratchets for wear.

Brake

1. Make sure the leading edge of each brake lining is tapered off for the first quarter of an inch. (If they are not, the ends may lift and cause a squealing noise.)
2. All rivets must be below the surface of the brake linings (17).
3. The linings for signs of wear or oil.

TO REASSEMBLE THE HUB

1. Prepare the following subassemblies:
    a. Fit the ball cage (23) into the driver (43), with the ring of the ball cage facing outwards and press in the dust cap (44), with the recess facing outwards (see Fig 55). If a new ball cage is used, the dust cap should also be new. If the sprocket has been removed, fit on the dust cap (46), washers (48) and sprocket (47)—in the same order noted on dismantling—and fix in position with circlip (49).
    b. Fit the balls (24 only) and the inner dust cap (42) into the right-hand ball ring (41) making sure that the balls can revolve freely with the dust cap in position.
    c. Fit the gear-ring pawls (40), pins (31), and springs (33) into the gear ring (39). (See Fig. 56).
    d. Smear grease in the channel of the dust cap (46). Do not use grease inside the hub.
2. Hold the axle (27/28) in a vise—with slot for axle key (52), above the sun pinion—and fit on the planet cage (34).
3. Add the planet pinions (35) and pins (36) (the small ends of the pins protrude).
4. Fit on the clutch sleeve (37), flange first, clutch (38), with the recess over the flange of the sleeve, axle key (52), with the flats facing upwards, and screw in the indicator coupling (57) or (58).
5. Locate thrust ring (53) over flats of axle key (52).
6. Fit gear ring (39) (subassembly B) over planet cage (34).
7. Position right-hand ball ring (41) on the gear ring (39).
8. Add the driver (43), complete with fittings (subassembly A).
9. Slide clutch spring (55), and cap (56), over the axle.
10. Screw on the right-hand cone (45), finger-tight, then slacken 180°—half a full turn—and lock in this position with the lock washer (50) and lock nut(8).
    Note: Cone must not be unscrewed more than half a turn as this would throw the gear mechanism out of adjustment.
11. Fit the low-gear pawls (32), pins (31), and springs (33), into planet cage (34) (see Fig. 57).

Fig. 55.   Driver assembly.

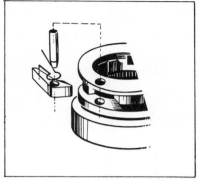

Fig. 56.   Pawl, pin, and spring fitted to gearing.

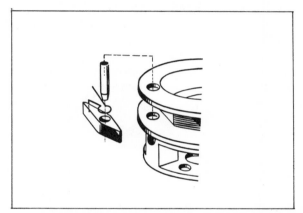

Fig. 57.   Pawl, pin, and spring fitted to planet cage.

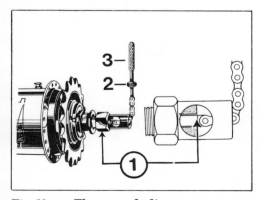

Fig. 58.   Three-speed adjustment on right side.

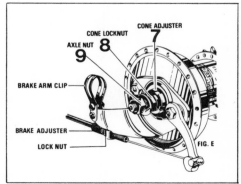

Fig. 59.   Brake adjustment on left side.

12. Screw the gear unit into the hub shell (24), or (25), and tighten ball ring (41).

13. Screw on left-hand cone (22), and fit on spacing washers (19) and (20).

14. Replace the brake plate (13), complete with shoes (18).
    Note: If the brake shoes have been removed, make sure that they are replaced as described below.

15. Fit on spacing washer (20), notched cone adjusting washer (7), spacing washer (11), and left-hand cone lock nut (8) (loosely).
    Adjust the hub bearing to ensure no play at the hub, but a trace of side play at the rim.

16. Fit wheel onto bicycle frame and add axle washers (10), axle nuts (9) and (51). Adjust gear.

GEAR CORRECTION GUIDE (3 SPEED HUB BRAKE)

Note: The major cause of trouble is faulty gear adjustment. Check to see that the end of the indicator rod is level with the end of the axle when gear control is in No. 2 position. If the complaint is sluggish gear change or stiffness, this may point to lack of oil.

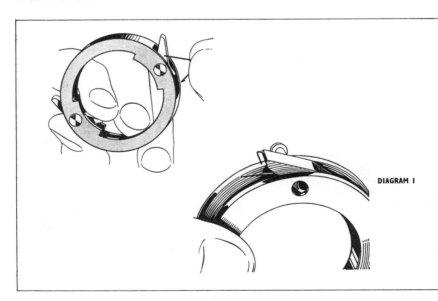

DIAGRAM I

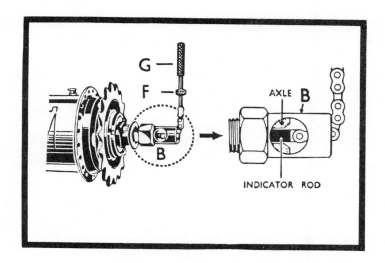

GEAR ADJUSTMENT
Push Gear Lever to No. 2 position and screw the wire connection (G) until the end of the indicator rod is exactly level with the extreme end of the axle. This can be seen through "window" in the right hand nut (see B) now tighten locknut (F). Should gears slip —check and readjust immediately.

TO REMOVE CONTROL WIRE
Remove centre screw (13) from plastic cover plate (9) —detach cover and remove old wire.

TO FIT WIRE
1.   Push control lever to No. 3 position and fit wire nipple into recess below control lever.
2.   Pass wire through slot of wire anchorage and over pulley wheel.
3.   Connect control wire to gear indicator at hub.
4.   Readjust gear.

Fig. 60.   Correct placement of pawl, spring, and pin in planet ring.

SYMPTOM	FAULT	REMEDY
Slipping in low gear (1st)	1. Sliding clutch worn	1. Replace
	2. Indicator not screwed in fully	2. Readjust
	3. R.H. cone incorrectly adjusted	3. Readjust
	4. Kinks in control wire	4. Replace
	5. Twisted indicator chain	5. Replace
Self-changing gear action between 1st gear and 2nd gear	1. Worn gear-ring pawls	1. Replace
	2. Worn ends of clutch	2. Replace
Slipping in normal gear (2nd)	1. Gear-ring dogs and/or clutch worn	1. Replace
Slipping in top gear (3rd)	1. Pinion pins and/or clutch worn	1. Replace
	2. Weak or distorted axle spring	2. Fit new spring
	3. Incorrect R. H. cone adjustment	3. Readjust
	4. Grit between clutch sleeve and axle	4. Clean
Hub runs stiffly	1. Too many ball bearings in ball ring	1. Fit in 24 only
	2. Cones too tight	2. Readjust
	3. Chainstay ends not parallel	3. Correct
	4. Corrosion	4. Clean and use S.A. oil
Sluggish gear change	1. Distorted axle spring	1. Replace
	2. Bent axle	2. Replace
	3. Worn indicator chain link	3. Replace

SYMPTOM	FAULT	REMEDY
	4. Lack of oil, or frayed wire	4. Oil or replace

BRAKE CORRECTION GUIDE

Inefficient brake	1. Oil-soaked or greasy linings	1. Fit new linings
	2. Incorrect adjustment	2. Readjust
	3. Worn linings; rivet heads protruding and contacting drum surface	3. Fit new linings
Squealing brake	1. Loose brake arm clip	1. Secure clip
	2. Linings not tapered off at front edge, causing vibration	2. Fit linings correctly
	3. Loose rivets in linings	3. Secure rivets firmly
Brake action irregular	1. Hub drum pulled out of shape during wheel building	1. Re-true wheel or rebuild as necessary
Knocking or clicking noise	1. Loose hub shell rivets	1. Fit new hub shell
	2. Scored brake drum surface	2. Fit new hub shell

BRAKE SHOE ASSEMBLY

Figure 61 illustrates the correct assembling of the brake shoes, but the following points should be specially noted:

It is important that brake shoes are reassembled so that the side of the brake cam with the largest flat area is on the inside, towards the axle (see letter A).

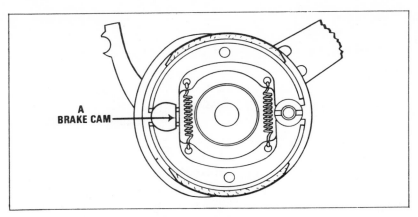

Fig. 61.   Internal view of expanding brake mechanism.

To allow both brake shoes to be applied evenly the cam is slightly offset, and if not fitted correctly will allow one shoe only to operate with consequent loss of brake efficiency. It is also important to ensure that the flange which carries the brake springs fits next to the brake arm plate.

GENERAL NOTES

Gear Ratios

1. The AB hub provides three gears. The direct drive is in normal gear. Top gear provides an increase of 33.33 percent and low gear a decrease of 25 percent from normal.
2. Sprockets: A range of sprockets from 14T to 22T is available for this hub.
3. It is important that the axle should be prevented from rotating in the chainstay slots and the flats on the axle are provided for this purpose. If the chainstay ends are too wide for the axle, special washers are supplied.
4. If the hub has been dismantled, check the gear indicator adjustment. Make sure that the gear indicator coupling is fully screwed into the axle key.

Bearing Adjustment (see Fig. 59)

Adjustment is made by left-hand cone (22), which projects through the brake plate. Loosen axle nut (9), cone lock nut (8), and slotted adjusting washer (7). Screw in cone finger tight, then adjust the hub bearing until there is no play at the hub, but a trace of side play at the wheel rim. The right-hand cone

(45), is set at the factory and should not be altered. However if the hub has been dismantled, reset this cone as follows (before adjusting the left-hand cone). Screw in cone finger tight only, then unscrew it counterclockwise 180°—half a turn—and lock in this position with lock washer (50) and lock nut (8).

Adjustment of Cable Operated Brakes (see Fig. 59)

To adjust, slacken lock nut and tighten adjuster so that the brake linings are in contact with the brake drum; then slacken adjuster until the wheel spins freely. Tighten lock nut. Occasionally check brake arm slip for tightness.

Adjustment of Rod Operated Brakes (see Fig. 59)

The principle of adjustment is exactly as described for cable brakes. The adjustment is controlled by a special knurled adjuster nut at the end of brake rod.

Brake Lining Renewals

If brake efficiency is impaired and cannot be corrected by adjustment, brake linings may be worn and need renewal. Dealer will arrange to reline brake shoes.

Gear Adjustment (see Fig. 58)

First, place the gear control in No. 2 position. Then screw the cable connector (3) until the end of the indicator rod is exactly level with the extreme end of the axle. This can be seen through the "window" in the right-hand nut (see 1). Now tighten lock nut (2). All gears are now set.

LUBRICATION

A New Hub Must Be Oiled Before Use

Lubrication of the bearings is made through lubricator in hub shell. *Use only Sturmey Archer Oil* (SAE 20), applying a few drops once a month. The brakes are designed to run dry. No oil must be allowed to reach the brake linings. The slot in the brake plate is provided to drain oil from hub bearing. This must be free from dirt. A spot of oil should occasionally be applied between the brake arm bushing and brake-arm lever.

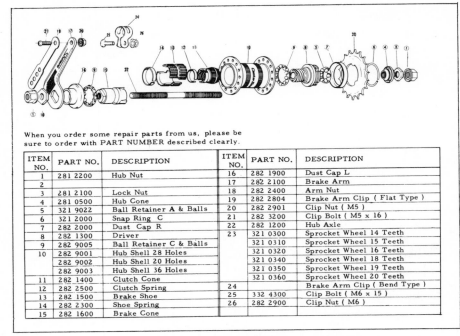

When you order some repair parts from us, please be
sure to order with PART NUMBER described clearly.

ITEM NO.	PART NO.	DESCRIPTION	ITEM NO.	PART NO.	DESCRIPTION
1	281 2200	Hub Nut	16	282 1900	Dust Cap L
2			17	282 2100	Brake Arm
3	281 2100	Lock Nut	18	282 2400	Arm Nut
4	281 0500	Hub Cone	19	282 2804	Brake Arm Clip (Flat Type)
5	321 9022	Ball Retainer A & Balls	20	282 2901	Clip Nut (M5)
6	321 2000	Snap Ring C	21	282 3200	Clip Bolt (M5 x 16)
7	282 2000	Dust Cap R	22	282 1200	Hub Axle
8	282 1300	Driver	23	321 0300	Sprocket Wheel 14 Teeth
9	282 9005	Ball Retainer C & Balls		321 0310	Sprocket Wheel 15 Teeth
10	282 9001	Hub Shell 28 Holes		321 0320	Sprocket Wheel 16 Teeth
	282 9002	Hub Shell 20 Holes		321 0340	Sprocket Wheel 18 Teeth
	282 9003	Hub Shell 36 Holes		321 0350	Sprocket Wheel 19 Teeth
11	282 1400	Clutch Cone		321 0360	Sprocket Wheel 20 Teeth
12	282 2500	Clutch Spring	24		Brake Arm Clip (Bend Type)
13	282 1500	Brake Shoe	25	332 4300	Clip Bolt (M6 x 15)
14	282 2300	Shoe Spring	26	282 2900	Clip Nut (M6)
15	282 1600	Brake Cone			

Fig. 62.   Exploded view of Shimano coaster brake.

SHIMANO COASTER BRAKE

The Shimano coaster brake works when a clutch is forced
against brake shoes causing them to expand and lock against
the brake hub of the bicycle as the brake is applied.

TO DISASSEMBLE

1. To disassemble the Shimano coaster brake, first use a wrench
   to loosen the lock nut and hub cone on the gear side, and
   remove them.
2. The driver with the sprocket wheel can be removed by turning
   the sprocket wheel counterclockwise.
3. The hub shell and internal mechanism can now be disassembled, so take the hub axle, containing the internal mechanism, out of the hub shell.
4. Next, remove the assembly of the clutch cone and brake
   shoe from the axle. The clutch cone can then be removed by
   pulling it out of the brake shoe.

Fig. 63.   Shimano coaster brake.

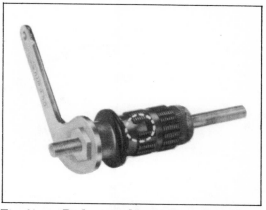

Fig. 64.   Brake assembly fitted into hub as seen from left side.

5. The brake cone, ball retainer, dust cap (L), and brake arm are assembled in the hub axle, but it is not necessary to disassemble them unless they are defective.

6. The method of disassembling these is to clamp the axle between the soft metal jaws of a vise (brake arm up), and loosen the arm nut with a wrench. Then remove the brake arm and take out the retainer.

7. If it should be necessary to disassemble the brake cone, loosen it from the hub axle and remove it.

8. This completes the instructions on disassembly. Be sure to clean each part carefully with oil.

TO ASSEMBLE

1. In case the brake cone and hub axle have been disassembled, screw the brake cone onto the hub axle from the side with the protruding parts. Note the following check points:
   a. Screw the brake cone onto the short thread part of the hub axle.
   b. Screw the brake cone all the way onto the hub axle.

2. Push in the ball retainer. Be sure that the balls are facing inside, otherwise the retainer might break.

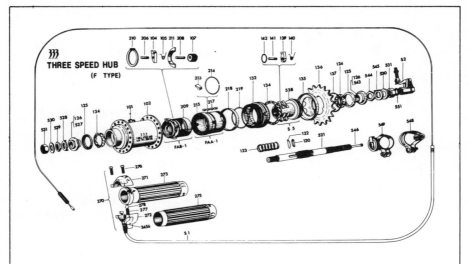

PART NO.	DESCRIPTION	PART NO.	DESCRIPTION
101	Lubricator	219	Snap Ring D
102	Hub Shell W/Left Cup	270	Grip Control Set
104	Pawl C	271	Upper Holder
105	Pawl Spring C	272	Lower Holder
107	Planet Pinion	273	Grip (right)
120	Sliding Key A	275	Grip (left)
122	Sliding Key B	276	Setting Screw
123	Spring	277	Grip Spring
124	Ball Retainer A	278	Ball
125	Dust Cap A	521	Axle
126	Dust Cap B	527	L. H. Cone W/Dust Cap B.
132	Ball Cup	528	Cone Stay Washer
134	Ball Retainer B	529	Lock Nut A
135	Dust Cap	530	Washer
136	Sprocket Wheel	531	Nut
137	Snap Ring C	538	Driver
139	Pawl B	543	R. H. Cone W/Dust Cap B.
140	Pawl Spring B	544	Lock Nut B
141	Pawl Pin B	545	Non-Turn Washer
142	Snap Ring B	546	Push Rod
206	Pawl Pin C	548	Stopper
208	Pinion Pin B	549	Guide Roller
209	Ratchet B-1	551	Bell Crank Lock Nut
210	Snap Ring A	FAA-1	Complete Ratchet A-1
211	Pawl Plate	FAB-1	Complete Ratchet B-1
213	Pawl A	S1	Complete Cable
214	Pawl Spring A	S2	Complete Bell Crank
215	Ratchet A	S5	Complete Driver
217	Roller	2456	Clamp Screw
218	Roller Cover		

Fig. 65.   Shimano three-speed hub (F type).

3. Put the dust cap (L) in place, fit the brake arm on the two-face part of the brake cone and tighten the lock nut.

4. When fitting the brake shoe onto the clutch cone, be sure that the clutch spring is facing in the proper direction, as shown in the illustration.

5. Adjust the clutch cone on the brake shoe so that the bent part of the clutch spring fits into the grooves of the brake shoe.
   Note: Apply sufficient grease to the brake shoe part.

6. Insert the completed assembly of the brake shoe into the brake cone. Make sure that the protruding part of the brake cone fits into the groove of the brake.

7. Assemble the hub shell by placing it over the brake shoe from the large side. Then push it so that the balls in the ball retainer fit properly to the hub. Be sure the balls are greased.

8. Screw the driver onto the hub shell to assemble it.

9. Finally, adjust the revolution of the hub with the lock nut and hub cone.
   Note: Do not loosen the lock nut on the brake arm side. If a large amount of play develops between the rim and the frame, adjust the hub revolution with the hub cone and lock nut on the gear side.

ATTACHING THE BRAKE TO FRAME

1. Fix the brake arm steady. To attach the hub to the frame, clamp the brake arm to the chain stay with the arm clip.

2. Next, place the lock washer on the hub axle and fasten it tightly with the hub nut.

Fig. 66.   Shimano three-speed hub.

SHIMANO THREE-SPEED HUB

The Shimano three-speed hub is an automatic hub. It can be shifted either while the bike is in motion or while standing still. It uses either a stick shift (as on a 20-inch bicycle) or a twist grip, which is used on adult bicycles and also on children's bicycles. There is a 33 percent gain from normal to high gear and a 25 percent drop from normal to low gear.

Figures 67 to 74 will show you how to assemble the three-speed hub.

Fig. 67.   Fit ratchet A-1 onto ratchet B-1 following the direction of the arrow.

Fig. 68.   Insert four rollers into each roller hole on ratchet A-1, then put the roller cover on, followed by the snap ring.

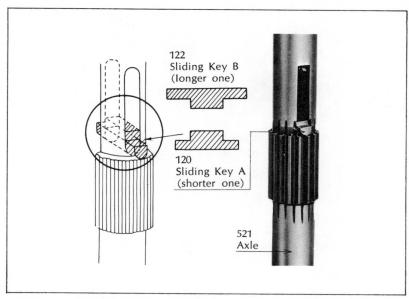

Fig. 69.   Insert sliding key (A) (shorter one) into the slot on the axle exactly as shown.

Fig. 70.   Fix the internal set to the axle slowly.

Fig. 71.   Insert sliding key (B) (longer one) into the slot on the axle as shown. After the internal parts are assembled, all rotating parts should be oiled fully.

Fig. 72.   Cover the internal parts with the hub shell as shown. Then assemble the clutch spring (123), L.H. cone with dust cap (527), cone stay washer (528), and lock nut (529). No threads are cut on the left cone. Tighten the lock nut firmly.

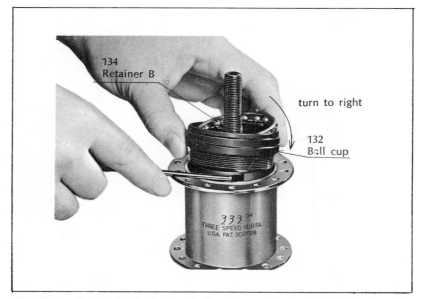

Fig. 73.   Screw the ball cup clockwise into the hub shell. Grease the retainer (B) well, and place it in the ball cup with the ball face down.

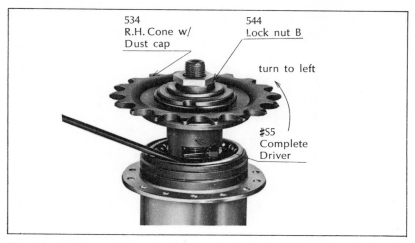

534
R.H. Cone w/
Dust cap

544
Lock nut B

turn to left

#S5
Complete
Driver

Fig. 74.   To assemble the driving body, press the pawls against the spring and insert the driving body into the hub shell easily. Use the push rod to hold the pawls against the spring, and rotate the driving body counterclockwise as shown.

REPAIRING SHIMANO THREE-SPEED

Cause of Trouble

Wear or damage of pawl (B) ("A" side).
Exchange it for a new one.
Wear or damage of pawl (B) ("B" side).
Exchange it for a new one.

Wear or damage of pawl (A), or pawl spring is too weak. Exchange rachet (A-1) for a new one and/or shorten the length of the spring a little to strengthen the spring action.

Wear or damage of pawl (C).
Replace it by taking off snap ring (A).

Oil shortage or rust to inner parts.
Clean all the parts and lubricate fully with No. 30 gear oil.

Breakage of retainer (A) or retainer (B).
Exchange them for well-greased new ones.

Local wear of sun gear. This will occur when the gear is used only at "H" position for a long time. Replace the axle.

Misadjustment of cable fitting. Loosen joint lock nut and adjust the indicator to point correctly along the line by turning joint at the "N" position of twist grip. Then tighten the joint lock nut. The same applies to click-stick.

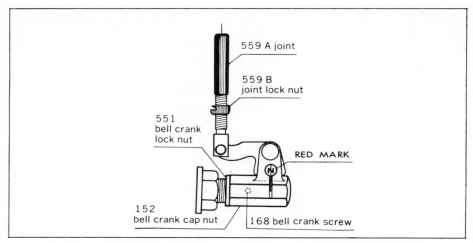

Fig. 75.   Bell crank in proper position in normal gear of three-speed hub.

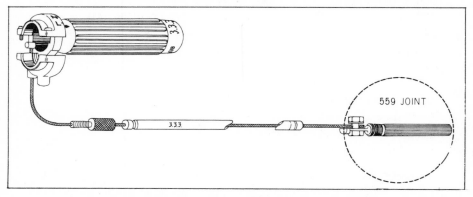

Fig. 76.   Twist grip control showing cable attachment.

Push rod (for correct length) will come about half an inch out of edge of axle. Do not loosen the bell crank set screw for it is the stopper to set the positon of bell crank.

In case the twist grip is felt heavy when twisting, draw the grip somewhat out from the handlebar and fasten the screw. In case it is felt too light when twisting, push and set the full length of the grip to the handlebar.

ADJUSTING CABLE TO BELL CRANK
ON SHIMANO THREE-SPEED HUB

When the twist grip is in the position of "N," the red circled "N" mark and the red line engraved on the bell crank should come to a precise position to be seen through the groove on the cap nut, as shown in Fig. 75.

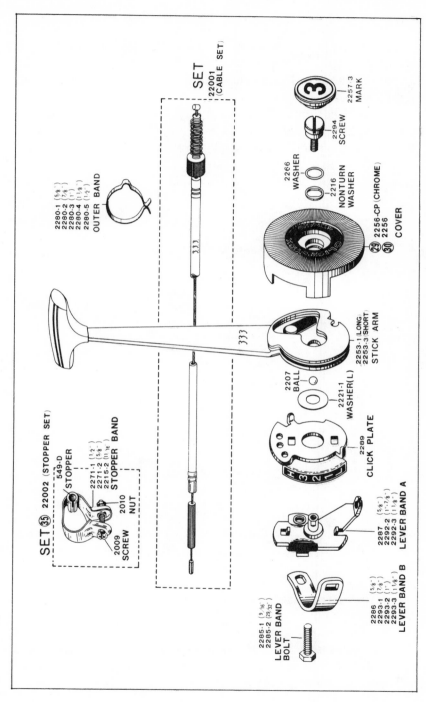

Fig. 77.   Exploded view of click-stick assembly.

HOW TO ATTACH CABLE TO GRIP OR CLICK-STICK

Attach the wire just as in the case of changing the wire of the grip control of the 3-speed hub. Pass the wire through the groove on universal joint and fasten it with nut in order to set joint (559A) to bell crank set.

Remove the joint bolt of repairing wire (Fig. 77). Replace adjusting bolt and adjusting spring (Fig. 78). Set universal joint to bell crank set as in grip control system.

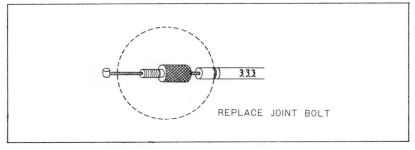

REPLACE JOINT BOLT

Fig. 78.   Cable end fitted to bell crank.

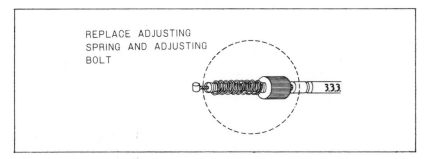

REPLACE ADJUSTING
SPRING AND ADJUSTING
BOLT

Fig. 79.   Cable end fitted to twist grip.

SHIMANO'S AUTOMATIC SPEED CHANGE

Features

1. The automatic mechanism is employed inside a five-speed derailleur and you can enjoy more comfortable riding by adopting this new component.

2. The starting speed is reduced automatically by 25 percent which ensures a safe and very light start of a bicycle.

3. The speed change-point can easily be selected in five stages (1, 2, 3, 4, and 5) matching the pedaling strength of the rider.

4. You can enjoy ten different speeds with a five-speed derailleur because of an additional automatic mechanism on the five-speed freewheel.

5. Since the gear is always in low when starting, starting at a light load (25 percent automatic speed reduction) is possible.

6. When the speed exceeds the speed previously set, the gear automatically changes from low to high.

7. When the speed drops below the speed previously set, the gear changes from high to low (to do it in this case, just cease pedalling for a short while).

8. There are five gear set points. Select the set point best suited to your pace, i.e., physical energy, leg strength, and road condition. (The gear ratio is always 0.75:1.)

SHIMANO DISC BRAKE

This brake is operated by means of a brake lever mounted on the handlebar. As the lever is squeezed, the braking discs squeeze against a metal disc, causing the wheel to lock.

THE AUTOMATIC 5 AND HOW IT OPERATES

This system can be shifted while pedalling, without any special technique or use of levers, in the same way as conventional five-speed gear systems.

FEATURES OF THE AUTOMATIC 5

1. The automatic part of the unit has a special speed shifting mechanism attached to the freewheel, which puts it in low position when starting.

2. Once the bike attains a certain speed, this automatic part shifts into high gear. The automatic shifting point can be adjusted according to your individual preference: simply insert your thumb and forefinger into the holes in the red ring (on the freewheel) and turn. At the same time, watch the needle through the window in the speed selector plate, and set it to any of the numbers from 1 to 5 (see Fig. 82).

Fig. 80.   **Automatic speed changer as mounted on rear wheel.**

If you turn the needle toward 1, the automatic shifting point will be lowered (i.e., the bike will shift at a slower speed), and if you turn it toward 5, the point will be raised. The relation between the needle position and shifting point is shown in the following chart:

Needle position	1	2	3	4	5
Uses	for long-distance cycling	for short-distance cycling	for bicycling to school or shopping, etc.	for ladies	for exercise; for steep slopes

Note: In case of bad road conditions, if the bike gets a violent shock, it can shift to high speed even though the shifting point has not yet been reached (the opposite—unwanted shifting to low speed—never occurs). In this case, stop pedalling for a time and the mechanism will shift to low speed again. Then it will operate normally.

Fig. 81.   Shimano disc brake.

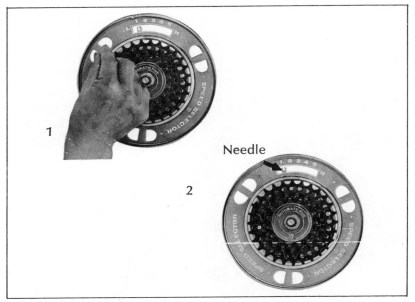

Fig. 82.   Manually changing gear ratio on automatic five-speed.

The shifting method is a speed loss type. The automatic high (normal) gear ratio is 1:1, and the low speed is 1:0.75, which makes it equivalent to the following number of teeth:

| High Speed | 15 | 17 | 20 | 25 | 30 |
| Low Speed | 20 | 22.6 | 26.6 | 33.3 | 40 |

For instance, if the automatic 5 is in low when the top gear (15 teeth) of the freewheel catches the chain, it is the same as if the chain catches a gear of 20 teeth at the start. But when it attains a certain speed it automatically changes to high (15 teeth).

AUTOMATIC 5 MAINTENANCE AND ADJUSTMENT

If there is no oil in the inner part of the gear shift wire, it will not work properly. Apply a little oil to the inside of the outer cover every two or three months.

Oil the derailleur about once a month with high quality machine oil, but not so much that it overflows. Wipe off all excess oil, because it will trap mud or dust and affect the working of the mechanism.

After about 2 weeks (more or less, depending on use), the wire will get loose. Adjust it to make the tension as tight as when it was new.

The inside of the Automatic 5 should always have sufficient oil. After purchasing, apply about 2 cc (½ teaspoon) of 30-weight motor oil, and do the same every six months. To oil, loosen the oil cap bolt on the right side of hub axle. Be careful not to apply too much oil.

SHIMANO THREE-SPEED COASTER BRAKE

The Shimano three-speed coaster brake, as the name implies, is a three-speed hub combined with a coaster brake. By a simple operation of the change lever, gears of the three-speed hub can be shifted to high, normal, or low. The coaster brake will operate to stop the bicycle if the pedal is revolved backward past a specified angle.

The new, improved point of this mechanism is that the structures of the three-speed hub and the coaster brake are completely independent, so that the coaster brake has no influence on the three-speed hub. This means that brake operation is more reliable, for greater safety.

KOMET SUPER COASTER BRAKE

The Komet coaster brake is actuated when the driving clutch (10) forces the brake cylinder to expand as the brake is applied. As the bicycle is being ridden, the driver (14) engages the driving clutch (10) and locks it against the hub wall.

TO DISASSEMBLE

1. Remove lock nut on brake arm side of hub (2).
2. Using the brake arm as leverage, unscrew stationary cone (7).
3. Remove wheel.
4. Remove brake cylinder and driving clutch (9 and 10) from wheel.
5. Remove driver (14).
6. Clean all parts with kerosene and wipe dry.

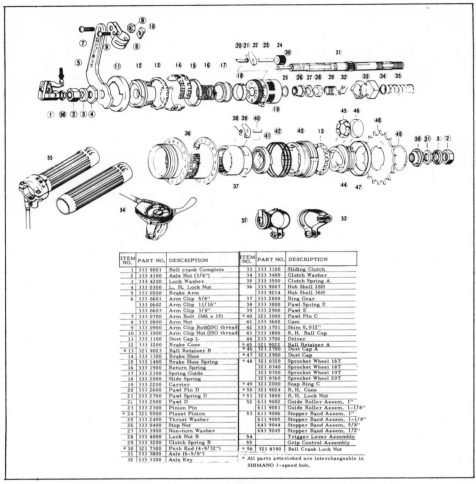

ITEM NO.	PART NO.	DESCRIPTION	ITEM NO.	PART NO.	DESCRIPTION
1	333 9001	Bell crank Complete	33	333 3100	Sliding Clutch
2	333 4100	Axle Nut (3/8")	34	333 3400	Clutch Washer
3	333 4200	Lock Washer	35	333 3500	Clutch Spring A
4	333 0300	L. H. Lock Nut	36	333 9007	Hub Shell 28H
5	333 0500	Brake Arm		333 9014	Hub Shell 36H
6	333 0601	Arm Clip 5/8"	37	333 2800	Ring Gear
	333 0602	Arm Clip 11/16"	38	333 3000	Pawl Spring E
	333 0603	Arm Clip 3/4"	39	333 2900	Pawl E
7	333 0700	Arm Bolt (M6 x 15)	* 40	321 1000	Pawl Pin C
8	333 0800	Arm Nut	41	333 3600	Cam
9	333 0900	Arm Clip Bolt(ISO thread)	42	333 1701	Shim 0.012"
10	333 1000	Arm Clip Nut (ISO thread)	43	333 1800	R. H. Ball Cup
11	333 1100	Dust Cap L	44	333 3700	Driver
12	333 1200	Brake Cone	* 45	321 9022	Ball Retainer A
* 13	321 9023	Ball Retainer B	* 46	321 2700	Dust Cap A
14	333 1300	Brake Shoe	* 47	321 2900	Dust Cap
15	333 1400	Brake Shoe Spring	* 48	321 0320	Sprocket Wheel 16T
16	333 1900	Return Spring		321 0340	Sprocket Wheel 18T
17	333 2100	Spring Guide		321 0350	Sprocket Wheel 19T
18	333 2200	Slide Spring		321 0360	Sprocket Wheel 20T
19	333 2200	Carrier	* 49	321 2000	Snap Ring C
20	333 2600	Pawl Pin D	* 50	321 9024	R. H. Cone
21	333 2700	Pawl Spring D	* 51	321 3800	R. H. Lock Nut
22	333 2500	Pawl D	52	611 9002	Guide Roller Assem. 1"
23	333 2300	Pinion Pin		611 9001	Guide Roller Assem. 1-1/8"
* 24	321 5500	Planet Pinion	53	611 9006	Stopper Band Assem. 1"
25	333 2400	Thrust Washer		611 9005	Stopper Band Assem. 1-1/8"
26	333 0400	Stop Nut		643 9044	Stopper Band Assem. 5/8"
27	333 3900	Non-turn Washer		643 9045	Stopper Band Assem. 1/2"
28	333 4000	Lock Nut B	54		Trigger Lever Assembly
29	333 3200	Clutch Spring B	55		Grip Control Assembly
* 30	321 7300	Push Rod (4-9/32")	* 56	321 8300	Bell Crank Lock Nut
31	333 3800	Axle (6-5/8")			* All parts asterisked are interchangeable in
32	333 3300	Axle Key			SHIMANO 3-speed hub.

Fig. 83.   Shimano three-speed coaster brake hub.

Fig. 84.   Shimano three-speed coaster brake.

TO REASSEMBLE

1. Place axle in vise up to cone attached to axle.
2. After greasing bearings inside of driver, place driver onto axle so that cone on axle rides on the bearings.
3. Place ball retainer (23) on driver and grease it, as well as the worm gear on the driver.
4. Place wheel over axle.
5. Insert brake cylinder and clutch assembly into wheel hub so that driving clutch engages the driver.
6. Pour a few drops of machine oil into hub.
7. Grease ball retainer on cone at arm side and thread cone onto the axle as far as it will go. Since the dogs (20) on the brake cylinder must be fitted into the slots of the cone, take the wheel out of the vise and turn the axle with your hand, holding the cone on the opposite side, until the dogs engage the slots of the cone. Keep turning the axle until side play is removed from the brake assembly.

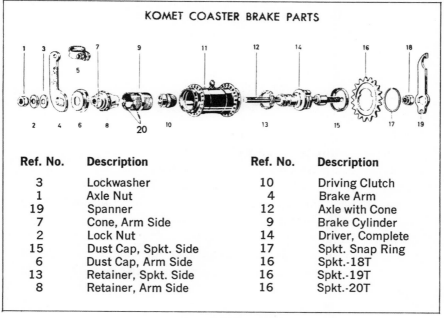

KOMET COASTER BRAKE PARTS

Ref. No.	Description	Ref. No.	Description
3	Lockwasher	10	Driving Clutch
1	Axle Nut	4	Brake Arm
19	Spanner	12	Axle with Cone
7	Cone, Arm Side	9	Brake Cylinder
2	Lock Nut	14	Driver, Complete
15	Dust Cap, Spkt. Side	17	Spkt. Snap Ring
6	Dust Cap, Arm Side	16	Spkt.-18T
13	Retainer, Spkt. Side	16	Spkt.-19T
8	Retainer, Arm Side	16	Spkt.-20T

Fig. 85.   Komet Super coaster brake.

8. Place wheel back in the vise on the sprocket side.
9. Place dust cap over cone.
10. Place brake arm into position on cone and lock in place with lock washer and lock nut.

SERVICING THE KOMET BRAKE

1. Brake does not stop quickly enough. (Check brake cylinder for wear or excess grease. If worn, replace cylinder.)
2. Brake grabs. (Brake cylinder is too dry. Oil it or put a light coat of grease on it, or replace brake cylinder.)
3. Pedals slip forward while riding. (Clutch worn, replace.)
4. Pedals slip backward when applying brakes. (Check dogs on brake cylinder. If broken, replace.)
5. Wheel locks. (Check cone adjustment. Make sure brake arm is securely locked in place with the lock nut, and brake arm is fastened to frame of bicycle with brake clip.)

CENTRIX COASTER BRAKE

The Centrix coaster brake is actuated when a clutch causes a four-piece brake sleeve to expand.

TO DISASSEMBLE

1. Place axle in vise on the brake arm side and remove sprocket cone.
2. Turn off sprocket and driver.
3. Lift wheel from the rest of assembly.
4. Remove driving clutch and brake sleeves.

Clean out all parts in kerosene and grease all bearings before reassembling. This type of coaster brake operates efficiently when properly adjusted. Bad adjustment (loose cones, loose lock nut on brake arm side) will cause the four-piece brake shoes to break. For proper adjustment, the wheel must spin freely without having any side play. Always make sure that the lock nut is tight against the brake arm and fastened securely against the bicycle frame with a brake clip.

NANKAI (NK) COASTER BRAKE

The NK coaster brake uses a three-piece clutch which is

forced against a series of 21 discs to actuate the brake. The discs in the brake are shaped so that every other one turns with the hub while the rest remain stationary. As the brake is applied, these discs squeeze against each other causing the wheel to stop.

TO DISASSEMBLE

1. Place axle in vise on brake arm side. Remove adjusting cone lock nut and adjusting cone.
2. Remove sprocket and driver assembly.
3. Remove wheel from rest of assembly.
4. Remove clutch assembly.
5. Remove discs from stationary cone.
6. Remove bearings. Clean all parts in kerosene.

TO ASSEMBLE

1. Grease bearings and place on stationary cone so that it rides freely on beveled surface of cone.
2. Place discs on stationary cone starting with a steel disc followed by a brass disc, and continue in this order until all the discs are in place.
3. Place the discs on the cone so that they will be perfectly in line.
4. Place stationary clutch on stationary cone.
5. Place spring on stationary cone so that the tongue of the spring will face up to fit into the slot of the sliding clutch.
6. Place sliding clutch with slot engaging brake spring.
7. Place wheel, with widest opening first, over assembly, being careful to engage all discs in slots of hub.
8. Place ball retainer in hub so that the widest part of retainer faces up.
9. Fit sprocket and driver assembly into the wheel. Grease bearings in sprocket assembly.
10. Thread adjusting cone onto the axle until finger tight.
11. Thread lock nut onto the axle up to the adjusting cone and lock in place against the adjusting cone, making sure the wheel spins freely without dragging the sprocket as it rotates. Also make sure that there is no side play.

REPAIRING NK COASTER BRAKE

If, when pedalling the bicycle, the pedals turn forward in a dragging manner without pulling the bicycle, replace the sliding clutch.

If the pedals slip backward when applying the brakes, replace the transfer spring on the stationary clutch.

If the brakes work poorly when applied, replace the set of discs on the stationary cone. If pedals slip forward and backward, the reason is usually a too loose adjustment of the adjusting cone and a broken transfer spring. When slippage occurs, it is also possible for the rectangular-shaped hole in the brake arm to be worn so that the stationary cone will turn. Always check to see that the brake arm is tight and in good condition.

TORPEDO COASTER BRAKE

The Torpedo coaster brake is almost an exact copy of the Komet coaster brake. It differs in that the hub shell is smaller and as a result the brake sleeve is smaller.

Follow the same instructions in servicing this brake as you would the Komet coaster brake.

Chapter IV

Derailleurs

DERAILLEURS—REAR

The purpose of the derailleur is to allow the bicycle rider a variety of gear ratios on the bicycle he is riding. By pushing or pulling a lever, the bicycle can be put into several different gear ratios. This change of gear ratios allows the rider to get maximum efficiency from the bicycle. He can travel at a high speed, or he can climb steep grades when he cuts the gear ratio down to approximately one-third of what he uses at the higher speed gears. With the wide variety of gears available on a derailleur-type bicycle, the rider can ride comfortably on almost any grade road on which a car can travel. Gear sprockets are available in sizes from 12-tooth up to 34-tooth for the back cluster, and from 36-tooth to 62-tooth for the front chain wheel. This gives the rider a wide range of gear ratios, from very high gear to very low gear.

GEAR TABLE 27" WHEELS														
	36	38	40	42	44	45	46	47	48	49	50	51	52	54
12	81.0	85.5	90.0	94.5	99.0	101.2	103.5	105.0	108.0	110.3	112.5	114.7	117.0	121.5
13	74.7	78.9	83.1	87.2	91.4	93.4	95.5	97.6	99.7	101.8	103.8	105.9	108.0	112.1
14	69.4	73.3	77.1	81.0	84.8	86.7	88.7	90.6	92.6	94.5	96.4	98.3	100.3	104.1
15	64.8	68.4	72.0	75.6	79.2	80.9	82.8	84.6	86.4	88.2	90.0	91.8	93.6	97.2
16	60.8	64.1	67.5	70.9	74.2	76.0	77.6	79.3	81.0	82.7	84.4	86.1	87.7	91.1
17	57.2	60.3	63.5	66.7	69.9	71.5	73.0	74.6	76.2	77.8	79.4	81.0	82.6	85.7
18	54.0	57.0	60.0	63.0	66.0	67.5	69.0	70.5	72.0	73.5	75.0	76.5	78.0	81.0
19	51.2	54.0	56.8	59.7	62.5	64.0	65.4	66.8	68.2	69.6	71.0	72.5	73.9	76.7
20	48.6	51.3	54.0	56.7	59.4	60.8	62.1	63.4	64.8	66.1	67.5	68.8	70.2	72.9
21	46.3	48.9	51.4	54.0	56.6	57.9	59.1	60.4	61.7	63.0	64.3	65.5	66.8	69.4
22	44.2	46.6	49.1	51.5	54.0	55.2	56.4	57.7	58.9	60.1	61.4	62.6	63.8	66.2
23	42.3	44.6	47.0	49.3	51.6	52.8	54.0	55.2	56.3	57.5	58.7	59.9	61.0	63.4
24	40.5	42.7	45.0	47.2	49.5	50.7	51.7	52.9	54.0	55.1	56.2	57.3	58.5	60.7
25	38.9	41.1	43.2	45.4	47.5	48.6	49.7	50.8	51.8	52.9	54.0	55.1	56.2	58.3
26	37.4	39.5	41.5	43.6	45.7	46.7	47.8	48.8	49.8	50.9	51.9	53.7	54.0	56.1

GEAR RATIOS NOT SHOWN ABOVE MAY BE CALCULATED AS FOLLOWS

$$\text{GEAR} = \frac{\text{Number of teeth on C/ring}}{\text{Number of teeth on Sprocket}} \times \text{Diameter of rear wheel in inches}$$

HOW THE DERAILLEUR WORKS

All derailleurs use the same principle for shifting the chain from one sprocket to another. When the shifting lever is actuated it causes the derailleur to open or close by means of a cable attached to the shifting lever on one end and to the derailleur on the other end. All derailleurs have adjusting screws which, when adjusted properly, prevent the derailleur from traveling too far in either direction. When the derailleur is out of adjustment it can cause the chain to go past either the top or bottom sprockets on the cluster, or it may not allow the chain to travel far enough to reach the top or bottom sprockets. It is most important to actuate the derailleur only when the sprocket chain is in motion. The movement of the sprocket chain is what causes the derailleur to operate when the shifting lever is used to change gears.

In order to get maximum efficiency from the derailleur, it is important that the front and rear sprockets are properly aligned. You will know that the sprockets are correctly aligned by placing a straight edge, such as a yard stick, flat against the inner side of the large front sprocket and seeing that it comes close to the third sprocket on a five-sprocket cluster. If it is off one-quarter inch or more in either direction, the chain will come off the front sprocket when the bicycle is in either high or low gear, depending upon which way the alignment is off.

CAMPAGNOLA NUOVA RECORD GEAR GHANGER

The Campagnola Nuova Record gear changer is a simple but well-constructed gear changer. It has the main body fastened to the gear fixing plate (which in turn is fastened to the frame of the bicycle), and two arms pivoting in and out from the gear fixing plate. At the bottom part of the main body is a cage containing 2 rollers which the chain runs through. This cage is spring-loaded in order to take up any slack in the chain as the chain is shifted from one sprocket to another. The main body of the derailleur is also spring-loaded at the point where the two arms are attached to the main body. This allows the derailleur to drop the chain to the smallest sprocket. The shifting lever and cable pull the cage and chain up to the larger sprockets when the shift is actuated. There are two adjusting screws attached to the derailleur. One adjusts the action of the pivoting arms so that the chain will not travel past the smallest sprocket on the cluster on the downward shifting motions, and the other adjusting screw stops the chain from traveling past the top sprocket on the cluster.

SERVICING THE CAMPAGNOLA NUOVA RECORD GEAR CHANGER

This type of derailleur requires very little servicing. A few drops of machine oil at the pivot joints and a little oil on the tension spring at the point where the cage is attached, plus some oil on the roller wheels every three months is sufficient to keep this derailleur in good operating condition for many years. Occasionally the tension spring will have to be replaced if the chain shows too much slack. This can be done by unscrewing the gear spring bolt (811A) and removing the spring (813A) from the other side of the gear body at the spring cage cover (812A) side.

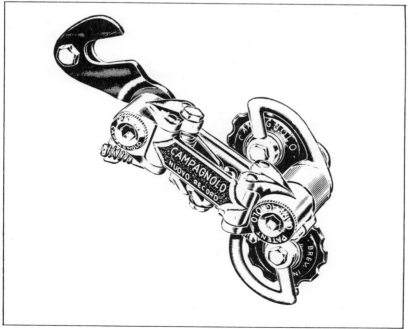

Fig. 86.   Campagnola Nuova Record gear changer.

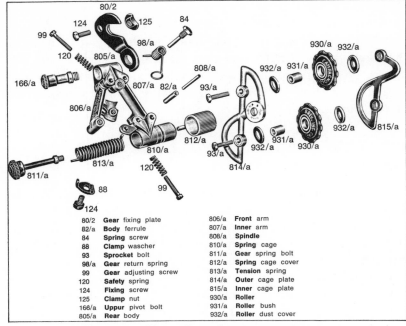

80/2	**Gear** fixing plate	806/a	**Front** arm
82/a	**Body** ferrule	807/a	**Inner** arm
84	**Spring** screw	808/a	**Spindle**
88	**Clamp** wascher	810/a	**Spring** cage
93	**Sprocket** bolt	811/a	**Gear** spring bolt
98/a	**Gear** return spring	812/a	**Spring** cage cover
99	**Gear** adjusting screw	813/a	**Tension** spring
120	**Safety** spring	814/a	**Outer** cage plate
124	**Fixing** screw	815/a	**Inner** cage plate
125	**Clamp** nut	930/a	**Roller**
166/a	**Uppur** pivot bolt	931/a	**Roller** bush
805/a	**Rear** body	932/a	**Roller** dust cover

Fig. 87.   Nuovo Record gear spare parts.

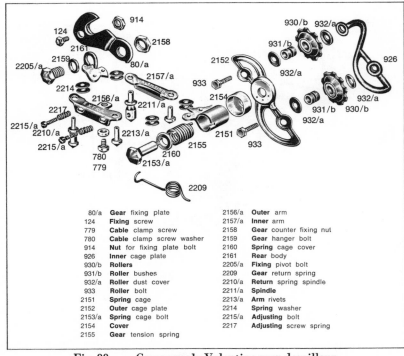

80/a	**Gear** fixing plate	2156/a	**Outer** arm
124	**Fixing** screw	2157/a	**Inner** arm
779	**Cable** clamp screw	2158	**Gear** counter fixing nut
780	**Cable** clamp screw washer	2159	**Gear** hanger bolt
914	**Nut** for fixing plate bolt	2160	**Spring** cage cover
926	**Inner** cage plate	2161	**Rear** body
930/b	**Rollers**	2205/a	**Fixing** pivot bolt
931/b	**Roller** bushes	2209	**Gear** return spring
932/a	**Roller** dust cover	2210/a	**Return** spring spindle
933	**Roller** bolt	2211/a	**Spindle**
2151	**Spring** cage	2213/a	**Arm** rivets
2152	**Outer** cage plate	2214	**Spring** washer
2153/a	**Spring** cage bolt	2215/a	**Adjusting** bolt
2154	**Cover**	2217	**Adjusting** screw spring
2155	**Gear** tension spring		

Fig. 88.   Campagnola Valentino rear derailleur.

CAMPAGNOLA VALENTINO EXTRA GEAR

The Campagnola Valentino extra gear changer is a light-weight derailleur built in such a way that all parts of it can be disassembled. It does not have the durability of the Nuova Record, but with proper care it will last many years. This derailleur also actuates from a pivot point directly below the mounting plate. It uses the same opening and closing action as the Nuova Record derailleur. Use same instructions for adjusting and lubricating this derailleur as the Nuova Record.

SIMPLEX PRESTIGE DERAILLEUR

This derailleur is a very smoothly operating unit. It uses a plastic body and plastic rollers. This derailleur also uses a pivot point just below the fastening bracket and opens and closes by means of a cable attached to the operating lever at one end and the derailleur at the other end. The derailleur is spring loaded at the base attached to the mounting bracket and also at the bottom of the derailleur where the gear cage is attached to the derailleur. A third coil spring is used for opening and closing the derailleur. This spring allows the bicycle chain to come down off the larger sprockets to the smallest sprocket. The upper spring (2973) forces the derailleur to move forward as the chain drops to the smaller sprockets. The lower spring (2974) keeps a constant tension on the gear gage. This tension keeps slack out of the bicycle chain in all gears.

Adjustments on the derailleur can be made on the adjusting screws (2979) so that the derailleur will move from the smallest sprocket to the largest without going past it, and back down to the smallest sprocket without going past that one. For smooth operation, apply a few drops of machine oil at the pivot points and to the rollers in the cage about every six months.

HURET DERAILLEURS

HURET LUXE TOURING #2100

The Hurt Luxe derailleur (Fig. 90) differs from most others in that the main body of the derailleur (2101) remains in a vertical position when it is actuated while the rest of the parts hinged to it open and close. The body (2101) will move forward and backward in a lateral position parallel to the frame of

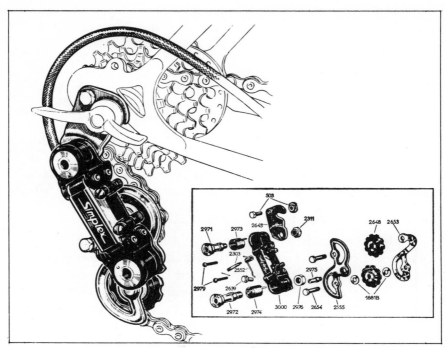

Fig. 89.   Simplex Prestige derailleur.

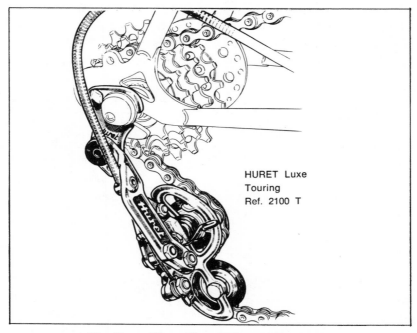

HURET Luxe
Touring
Ref. 2100 T

Fig. 90.   Huret "Luxe" Touring derailleur.

the bicycle, as the chain moves up or down the sprockets. The hinging mechanism (2118) is spring loaded for bringing the derailleur down from the top sprockets, and the cage assembly (2131 and 2132) is spring loaded for keeping slack out of the bicycle chain. Adjustments on this derailleur can be made by tightening or loosening adjusting screws (2125 and 2123) so that the derailleur will not travel past the largest sprocket going up, or past the smallest sprocket going down. If more tension is desired on the roller cage, the tension spring (2152) can be moved forward to a tighter position. Occasionally dirt or sand can become lodged at the pivot point of the derailleur which causes the derailleur to not drop down freely off the top sprockets. This can be remedied by loosening screws (2118 and 2113) about a half turn. A few drops of machine oil every three months at all pivot points and on the cage rollers will help to keep this derailleur operating efficiently.

HURET LUXE SUPER-TOURING DERAILLEUR #2100 ST

This derailleur is made exactly like the Huret Luxe derailleur except that the cage and roller mechanism is approximately one inch longer (see Fig. 91). This extra length allows more tension on the bicycle chain and wider range of sprockets.

HURET ALLVIT DERAILLEUR

The Huret Allvit derailleur (Fig. 92) differs from the Luxe models in that it has a strongly built main body to which all of the moving components are attached. As the derailleur is actuated, all the hinged parts move to get the chain up or down the sprockets. It is important to have all moving parts lubricated, including the cable core running through the cable housing in order to allow the derailleur to operate freely. The roller cage (2131 and 2132) is spring loaded to allow tension on the chain and the derailleur. The tension spring (1912) allows the derailleur to come down off the larger sprockets to the smallest one. The adjusting screws (1914 and 1916) prevent the chain from traveling too far in either direction. If at times the derailleur fails to come down from the larger sprockets, loosen screws (1907, 1908, and 1909) about one-half turn.

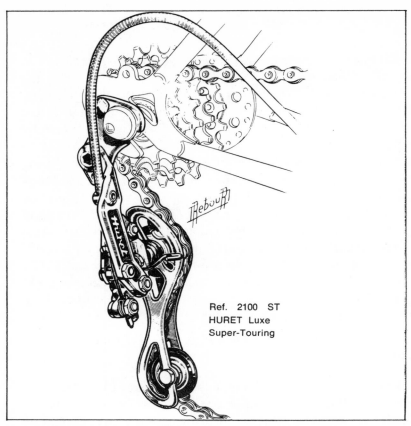

Ref. 2100 ST
HURET Luxe
Super-Touring

Fig. 91.   Huret Luxe Super-Touring derailleur.

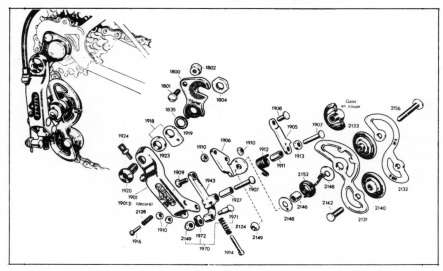

Fig. 92.   Huret Allvit derailleur.

HURET ALLVIT DERAILLEUR WITH CABLE SAVER

This model is identical to the Standard Model 7900 except that the adjusting barrel (1924) is spring loaded to remove some of the slack from the cable as it is actuated.

HURET SVELTO DERAILLEUR

The Svelto derailleur (Fig. 93) differs from the other Huret derailleurs in that the main body (2001) pivots back and forth with the roller cage as the derailleur is actuated. It is spring loaded (2017) to bring the chain down off the larger sprockets and uses a spring (2152) to keep tension on the bicycle chain as it runs through the roller cage (2131 & 2132). Adjustments to keep the chain from traveling too far can be made with adjusting screws (1916). Oil all moving parts with machine oil every three months.

HURET JUBILEE DERAILLEURS

Models #2200, 2252, and 2240 are basically alike. They differ only in length of the roller cage in order to accommodate clusters of sprockets such as 13 to 24 teeth for model #2200, 13 to 28 for model #2252, and for special Italian fork-end fittings on model #2240.

This derailleur differs from the Huret Allvit in that it is an alloy derailleur which is considerably lighter in weight than the Allvit. The operating principle is also completely different. Although the "Jubilee" derailleur is fastened to the bicycle frame in the same manner as the Allvit, upon actuating the derailleur the main body swings back and forth from a point just below the point of attachment. This allows a freer movement, and also allows the chain, riding on the rollers in the roller cage, to be directly under the sprocket that it is being used for. With this pivotal action, it takes less effort to actuate this derailleur than the Allvit model.

HURET JUBILEE DERAILLEUR—MODELS #2248, 2253, AND 2254

This derailleur is the same as models #2200, 2252, and

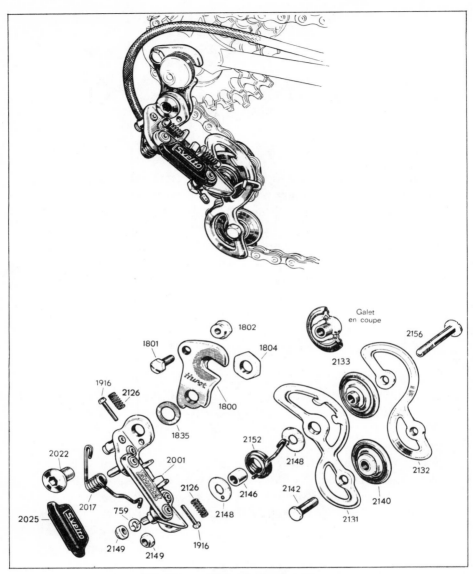

Fig. 93.   Huret Svelto derailleur.

2240, except that the roller cage is longer, which allows the use of larger cluster gears, up to and including 30 teeth.

Adjusting screws for controlling the travel of the roller cage are on the rear side of the derailleur and are easily accessible. Both models of the "Jubilee" derailleur are spring loaded so that the chain will come down off the larger sprockets as tension is released on the cable attached to them and to the hand lever.

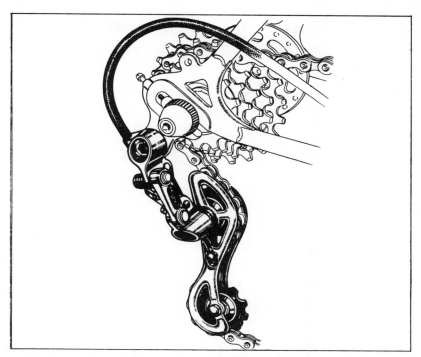

Fig. 94.   Huret Jubilee rear derailleur, models 2200, 2252, and 2240.

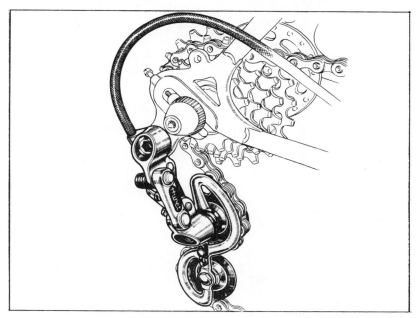

Fig. 95.   Huret Jubilee derailleur, models 2248, 2253, and 2254.

Fig. 96.   Huret Jubilee front derailleur, model 500.

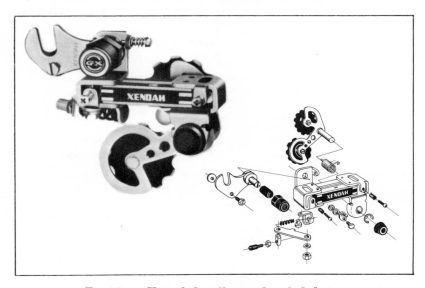

Fig. 97.   Xenoah derailleur and exploded view.

RD 16 "FBM TRAIL"
REAR DERAILLEUR

Fig. 98.   Danube derailleur.

FRONT JUBILEE DERAILLEUR—MODEL 500

The model 500 "Jubilee" front derailleur is an alloy derailleur. It is sturdily constructed and uses rivets at all pivot positions. It is spring loaded to come down to the smaller front sprocket as tension is released on the shifting cable. The mechanical principle used allows for smooth and easy operation.

THE XENOAH "DANUBE" DERAILLEUR

This is a new derailleur from Japan that is made by Xenoah Co. It is well constructed and is operated in a pivotal manner, where the main body swings in and out as the derailleur is activated. It is spring loaded to come down off the larger sprockets, and the roller cage is spring loaded to keep tension on the bicycle chain at all times. Adjusting screws are located on the rear side of the main body to prevent the roller cage from traveling too far in either direction.

THE "DANUBE" DERAILLEUR—MODEL RD 16

The Xenoah derailleur and the "Danube" are similar in construction and operation. They differ in that the "Xenoah" derailleur has an additional adjustment for chain placement and tension that the other derailleurs made by this company do not have. This adjusting screw is placed near the mounting bracket, and allows the roller cage to be moved back as the adjusting screw is tightened. This puts more tension on the bicycle chain.

SHIMANO LARK DERAILLEUR

The Shimano Lark (Figs. 99 and 100) is a conventional derailleur. The adapter (3) is fastened to the frame of the bicycle and the entire derailleur pivots at the link assembly (28) to actuate the bicycle chain. The link assembly is spring loaded so that the derailleur will move down from large sprockets as the chain is shifted from one sprocket to another. The chain is forced up from the smallest sprocket by the lever control as tension is put on the shifting cable. The roller cage assembly (24 and 20) is also spring loaded to keep proper tension on the chain. Adjustments can be made to prevent the chain from traveling too far in either direction by loosening and tightening screws (9). A few drops of oil every three months on all pivot-

Fig. 99.   Shimano Lark rear derailleur.

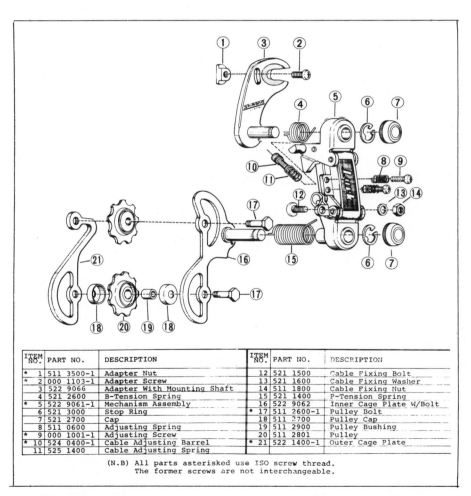

ITEM NO.	PART NO.	DESCRIPTION	ITEM NO.	PART NO.	DESCRIPTION
* 1	511 3500-1	Adapter Nut	12	521 1500	Cable Fixing Bolt
* 2	000 1103-1	Adapter Screw	13	521 1600	Cable Fixing Washer
3	522 9066	Adapter With Mounting Shaft	14	511 1800	Cable Fixing Nut
4	521 2600	B-Tension Spring	15	521 1400	P-Tension Spring
* 5	522 9061-1	Mechanism Assembly	16	522 9062	Inner Cage Plate W/Bolt
6	521 3000	Stop Ring	* 17	511 2600-1	Pulley Bolt
7	521 2700	Cap	18	511 2700	Pulley Cap
8	511 0600	Adjusting Spring	19	511 2900	Pulley Bushing
* 9	000 1001-1	Adjusting Screw	20	511 2801	Pulley
* 10	524 0400-1	Cable Adjusting Barrel	* 21	522 1400-1	Outer Cage Plate
11	525 1400	Cable Adjusting Spring			

(N.B) All parts asterisked use ISO screw thread.
      The former screws are not interchangeable.

Fig. 100.   Shimano Lark rear derailleur parts list and exploded view.

ing parts plus on the cage assembly and on the rollers will keep this derailleur in good operating condition.

SHIMANO EAGLE DERAILLEUR

The Shimano Eagle derailleur (Fig. 101) is very similar to the Lark derailleur. It differs in that it has a built-in steel guard that shields the derailleur from any outside damage. This derailleur, as well as the Lark, is designed so that the cage pulley wheels are always kept at a specified distance from the sprocket teeth of any gear. This makes the derailleur easier to use and more smoothly operating. The derailleur adjusts the same way as the Lark. Follow same instructions for oiling as the Lark derailleur.

THE SHIMANO CRANE DERAILLEUR

The Shimano Crane Derailleur (Fig. 103) is a completely new derailleur in the Shimano family. It is constructed of light alloy and is very smooth in operation. It is spring loaded to keep the chain on the smallest sprocket of the rear cluster and moves up to the largest sprocket with little effort. It has two adjusting screws to keep it from "overshifting" in either direction.

The main body pivots from the point of attachment. This allows smooth gear changing. The construction of this derailleur should give it a long and trouble-free life.

SUN TOUR DERAILLEUR

The Sun Tour derailleur (Fig. 104) differs from most other derailleurs in that it uses a slant pantograph mechanism. This means that the pulley cage assembly will always be on a parallel line with the sprockets as it is shifted from one sprocket to another. This type of operation allows very smooth shifting of the chain from one sprocket to the other. An angle adjusting screw (A) allows the main body of the derailleur to be parallel to the chain stay of the bicycle. When the chain is on the smallest sprocket, adjust the derailleur by using adjusting screw (C) so that the chain pulley is directly under it. After shifting to the top sprocket, make sure that the pulleys are directly under it by adjusting set screw (F). This derailleur is also spring loaded for lateral travel and in-and-out travel to the sprocket. Lubricate all moving parts every three months for ease of operation.

Fig. 101.   Shimano Eagle rear derailleur.

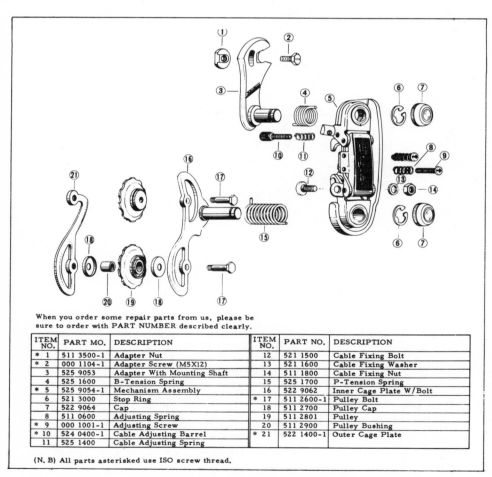

When you order some repair parts from us, please be sure to order with PART NUMBER described clearly.

ITEM NO.	PART MO.	DESCRIPTION	ITEM NO.	PART NO.	DESCRIPTION
* 1	511 3500-1	Adapter Nut	12	521 1500	Cable Fixing Bolt
* 2	000 1104-1	Adapter Screw (M5X12)	13	521 1600	Cable Fixing Washer
3	525 9053	Adapter With Mounting Shaft	14	511 1800	Cable Fixing Nut
4	525 1600	B-Tension Spring	15	525 1700	P-Tension Spring
* 5	525 9054-1	Mechanism Assembly	16	522 9062	Inner Cage Plate W/Bolt
6	521 3000	Stop Ring	* 17	511 2600-1	Pulley Bolt
7	522 9064	Cap	18	511 2700	Pulley Cap
8	511 0600	Adjusting Spring	19	511 2801	Pulley
* 9	000 1001-1	Adjusting Screw	20	511 2900	Pulley Bushing
* 10	524 0400-1	Cable Adjusting Barrel	* 21	522 1400-1	Outer Cage Plate
11	525 1400	Cable Adjusting Spring			

(N. B) All parts asterisked use ISO screw thread.

Fig. 102.   Shimano Eagle rear derailleur parts list and exploded view.

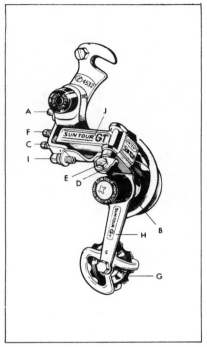

Fig. 103.   Shimano Crane derailleur.   **Fig. 104.**   Sun Tour GT derailleur.

FRONT DERAILLEURS

Although there are many different front derailleurs that are used to shift the chain from one crank sprocket to the other, they all use a chain guide that is actuated by a hand lever and cable. As the lever is pulled back, the cable attached to the derailleur forces the chain guide to move the chain from one sprocket to the other. There are adjusting screws to prevent the chain guide from moving too far in either direction. It is important to keep the front derailleur well lubricated for efficient operation. Some of the more popular derailleurs showing adjusting screws and points to oil are illustrated in Figs. 105 to 111.

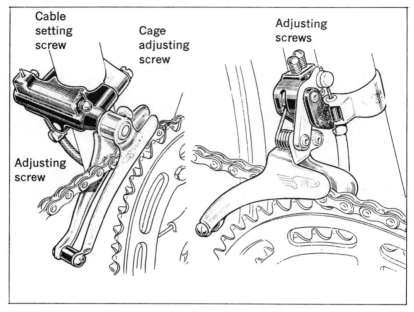

Fig. 105.   Simplex front derailleur.

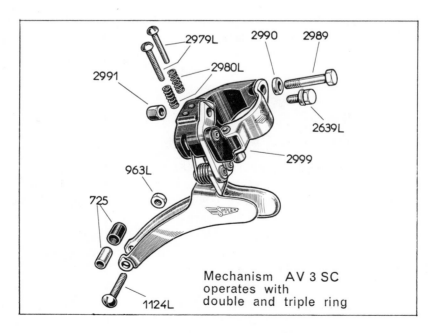

Fig. 106.   Simplex front derailleur.

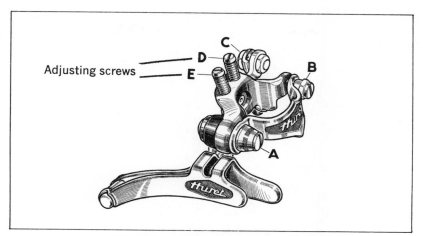

Fig. 107.   Huret front derailleur.

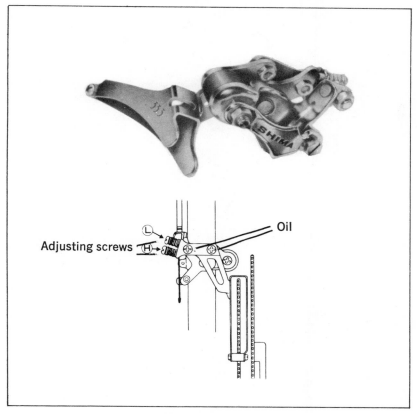

Fig. 108.   Shimano Lark.

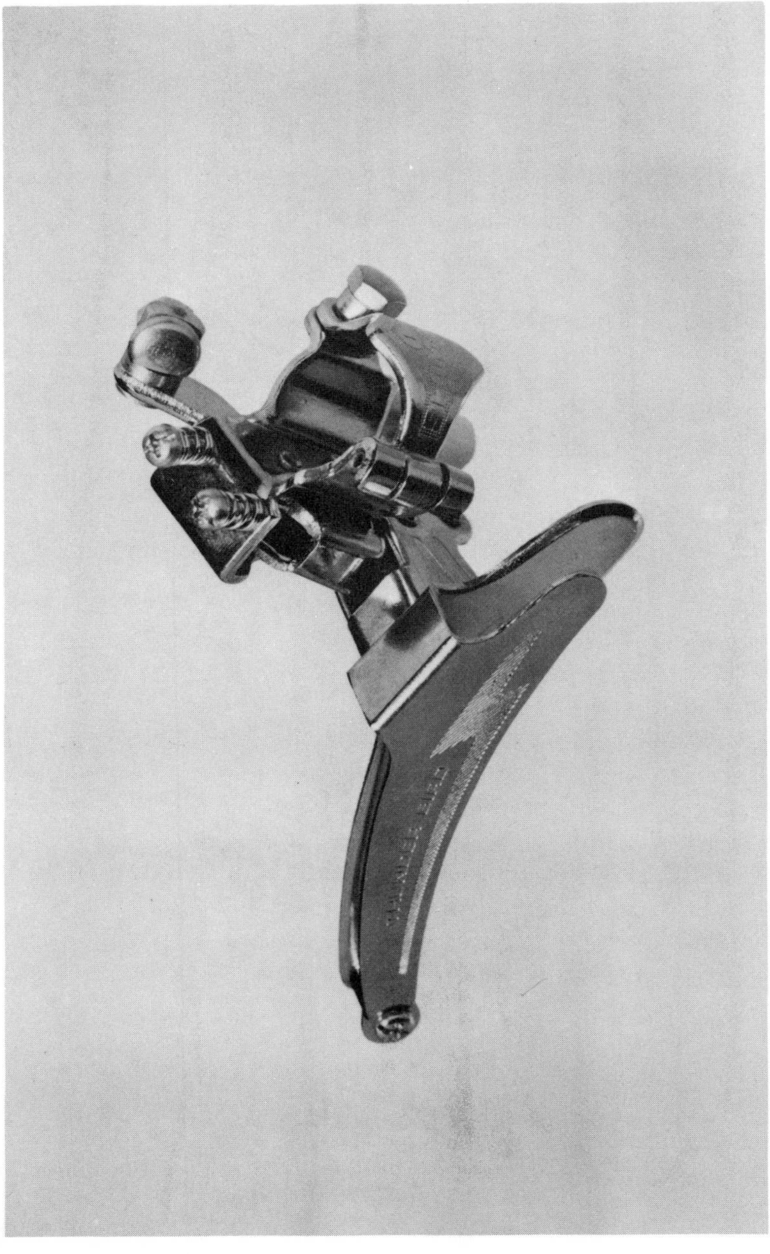

Fig. 109.   Shimano Thunder Bird.

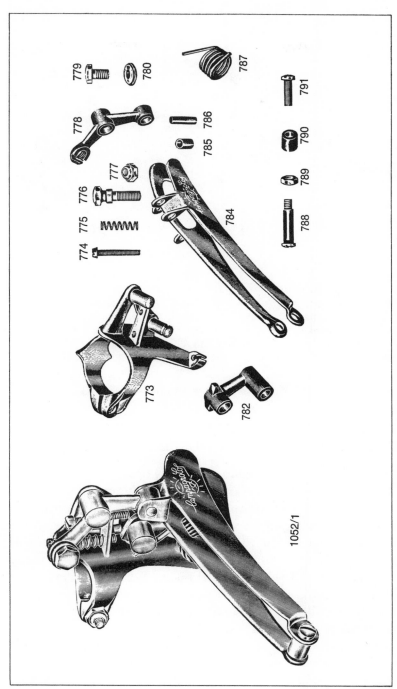

779 780 787 791 778 786 785 790 777 789 776 775 788 774 784 782 773 1052/1

Fig. 110.   Campagnola Nuovo Record front changer.

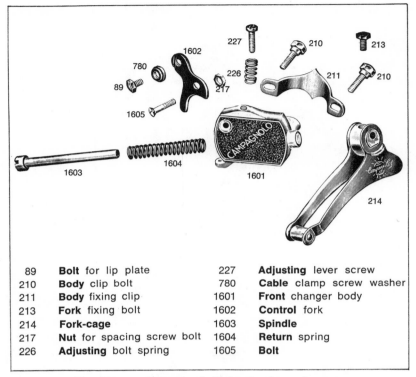

89	**Bolt** for lip plate		227	**Adjusting** lever screw
210	**Body** clip bolt		780	**Cable** clamp screw washer
211	**Body** fixing clip		1601	**Front** changer body
213	**Fork** fixing bolt		1602	**Control** fork
214	**Fork-cage**		1603	**Spindle**
217	**Nut** for spacing screw bolt		1604	**Return** spring
226	**Adjusting** bolt spring		1605	**Bolt**

Fig. 111.   Campagnola Valentino front changer.

GENERAL INFORMATION ON THE CARE AND MAINTENANCE OF REAR DERAILLEURS

The most important thing to do for easy operation of derailleurs is to make sure that they are working freely and that they are properly aligned with the sprockets. Also, check to see whether there is any binding in the shifting cables. A little grease on the cables where they fit into the cable housing will help for ease of operation. There are times when a bicycle is ridden in a sandy area and sand will get on the derailleur. When this happens, it will usually cause sluggishness in the derailleur movement. Remove the derailleur from the bicycle and clean it with kerosene. Also, weak spring action will cause a derailleur to malfunction. If you can dismantle it, you can do a better cleaning job. To reassemble, follow the picture guide in this chapter on that particular derailleur. Always lubricate all moving parts with a lightweight machine oil. If there is no adjustment on the spring, replace it with a new one. When a derailleur becomes bent, it will throw the rollers in the cage out of line with the sprockets on the cluster. When this happens, check carefully to find which part or parts are bent. If possible, remove these parts and straighten them, or replace them if they cannot be straightened.

Loose or too-tight cables will also cause malfunction of the derailleur. When adjusting derailleur cables put the bicycle chain on the smallest sprocket and pull the cable through the cable locking bolt until it is finger tight. Always check the fastening bolt that holds the derailleur to the bicycle frame to make sure it is tight. On Huret Allvit derailleurs there is a tendency for the derailleur to misfunction even when it is new. When the chain is on the top sprocket and it will not drop down to the smaller sprockets, loosen the nuts and bolts on the parts of the derailleur that open and close as the derailleur travels up and down the sprockets. Loosen the bolts about half a turn and lock them in that position with the nuts on them. This will free the derailleur.

If the derailleur is functioning properly and yet throws the chain off either of the front sprockets, check the frame alignment.

CARE AND MAINTENANCE OF FRONT DERAILLEURS

Front derailleurs, although a much simpler mechanism than rear derailleurs, usually cause malfunction when shifting from the smaller sprocket up to the larger sprocket if the derailleur is not set properly. Always try to have the derailleur fastened to the seat tube so that the chain cage comes as close to the top sprocket as possible without actually touching it when shifted to that position. The bicycle chain has a tendency to shift past the larger sprocket if the derailleur is mounted to high up on the seat tube. When the derailleur is mounted in the proper position and it still throws the chain too far, adjust it so that the chain is barely able to climb up to the top sprocket and bend the chain cage, where the chain hits it when shifting, so that it will force the chain to travel further when shifted to the top sprocket. This will help to make shifting smoother without too much chain grinding or over-shifting. There are times when the chain will not come down off the top sprocket when shifting to the smaller sprocket. This can be caused by a dirty mechanism, causing the derailleur to stick, or screws being too tight on a lever action derailleur such as Huret. This can be remedied by cleaning and loosening the screws about a half-turn on the actuating levers.

SHIFTING MECHANISMS

STURMEY ARCHER TRIGGER CONTROL

The Sturmey Archer trigger control (Fig. 112) is mounted on the handlebar, preferably on the right side close to the handlebar grip. This is a three-speed trigger. In the following illustration, the trigger lever is in normal gear (2), when shifted up, it is in high gear (3), and down it is in low gear (1). To get a correct adjustment on the gears, check the indicator rod by sighting it through the axle nut (B). When trigger handle is in (2), or normal gear, the end of the indicator rod should be even with the end of the axle. If it is not in this position, it can be adjusted by rotating the knurled connection (G) at the end of the shifting cable. When knurled connection is properly set, tighten nut (F) against it. This will keep it in proper alignment.

When replacing shifting cable in trigger, feed end of cable into opening (B) on trigger. When it is in high gear as cable moves through opening (B) move trigger slowly to low gear and at the same time apply pressure on the cable to force it into position (D). After cable is properly seated, keeping tension on the cable with one hand, push trigger back to high gear (3). Now feed cable through fulcrum clip (attached to top tube of bicycle and through pulley assembly) and attach to indicator chain.

STURMEY ARCHER TWIST GRIP CONTROL

Figure 114 shows the twist grip control disassembled. When replacing shifting cable, make sure that the spring (7) and ball bearing (6) are properly seated. It is the ball bearing under tension of the spring that allows the gears to be shifted automatically from one gear to the other. It is important to keep the fixing screws (8) tight at all times to prevent the ball bearing from falling out of place.

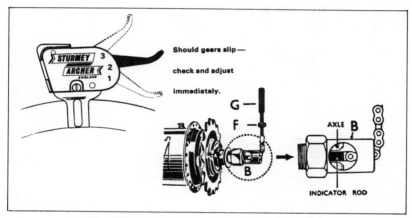

Fig. 112.   Sturmey Archer trigger control.

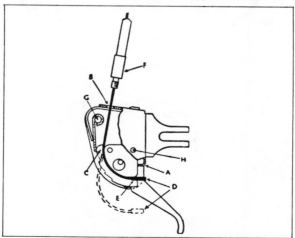

Fig. 113.   Feeding shifting cable into trigger control.

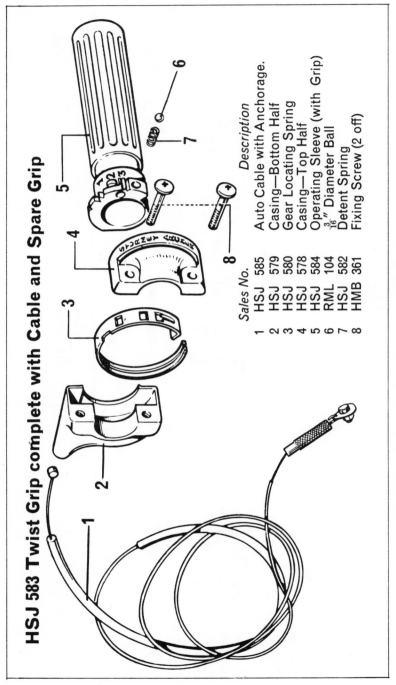

HSJ 583 Twist Grip complete with Cable and Spare Grip

Sales No.		Description
1	HSJ 585	Auto Cable with Anchorage.
2	HSJ 579	Casing—Bottom Half
3	HSJ 580	Gear Locating Spring
4	HSJ 578	Casing—Top Half
5	HSJ 584	Operating Sleeve (with Grip)
6	RML 104	$\frac{3}{16}''$ Diameter Ball
7	HSJ 582	Detent Spring
8	HMB 361	Fixing Screw (2 off)

Fig. 114.   Sturmey Archer twist grip assembly for three-speed hub.

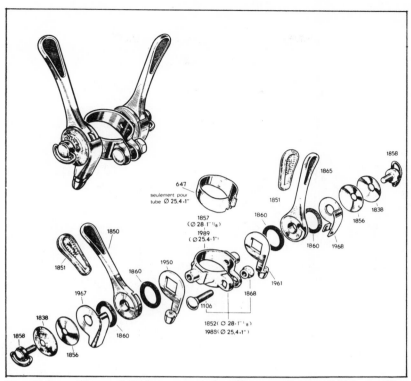

Fig. 115. Huret shift lever controls. When replacing shifting cable, replace all parts as shown in diagram.

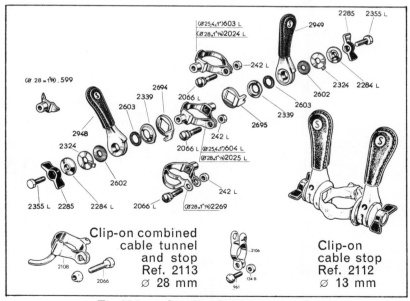

Fig. 116. Simplex shift lever control.

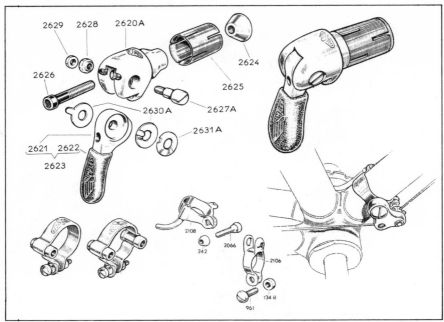

Fig. 117.   **Simplex handlebar control levers.**

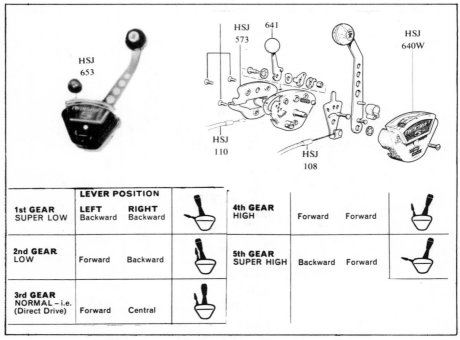

	LEVER POSITION						
1st GEAR SUPER LOW	**LEFT** Backward	**RIGHT** Backward		**4th GEAR** HIGH	Forward	Forward	
2nd GEAR LOW	Forward	Backward		**5th GEAR** SUPER HIGH	Backward	Forward	
3rd GEAR NORMAL – i.e. (Direct Drive)	Forward	Central					

Fig. 118.   **Sturmey Archer five-speed controls.**

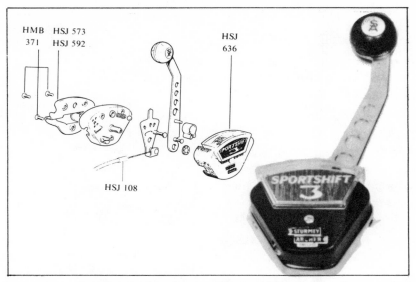

Fig. 119.   Sturmey Archer three-speed sportshift. Follow the same instructions for adjusting this shifting lever as for the Sturmey Archer five-speed controls.

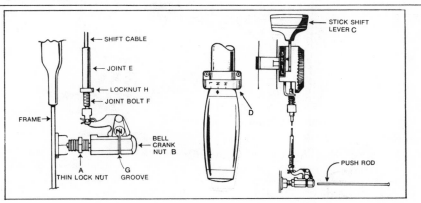

ADJUSTMENT INSTRUCTIONS FOR "3.3.3." 3-SPEED BICYCLES: (See Fig. 5) Insert push rod into right side of rear hub. Screw small thin lock nut (A) all the way onto axle. Screw bell crank nut (B) onto axle **until slight resistance is felt.** DO NOT FORCE BELL CRANK NUT ON ANY FURTHER. If bell crank joint bolt (F) does not line up with the shift cable, **unscrew bell crank nut** (½ turn) until it does. Push **stick shift lever (C)** to its most forward position (3 or H) or if equipped with twist grip (D), turn it to (3 or H). This lengthens the shift cable. Attach end of shift cable

Joint (E) to joint bolt (F). After making a few turns on the tightening joint (E), move hand control or twist grip control to position N or 2. In the bell crank nut there is a groove (G) and inside is a red line. The red line must be centered in the groove, and this is done by tightening or loosening the tightening joint (E). After aligning red line, secure with lock nut (H). Also lock bell crank nut into position by unscrewing thin lock nut (A) (already on rear axle) until tight against bell crank nut.

Fig. 120.   Shimano three-speed Twist Grip.

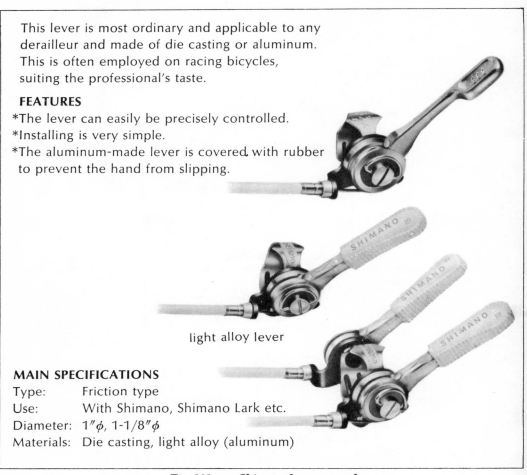

This lever is most ordinary and applicable to any derailleur and made of die casting or aluminum.
This is often employed on racing bicycles, suiting the professional's taste.

FEATURES
*The lever can easily be precisely controlled.
*Installing is very simple.
*The aluminum-made lever is covered with rubber to prevent the hand from slipping.

light alloy lever

MAIN SPECIFICATIONS
Type: Friction type
Use: With Shimano, Shimano Lark etc.
Diameter: 1″φ, 1-1/8″φ
Materials: Die casting, light alloy (aluminum)

Fig. 121.   Shimano lever controls.

CAMPAGNOLA HANDLEBAR TIP CONTROLS

The Campagnola handlebar tip controls are installed into the handlebar ends by tightening screw (137) through part (200/2). This causes expander shell (138) to tighten against inside of handlebars so that it locks firmly in place. Attach cable to hand lever (201) and fasten lever to part (200/2) securely with screw (140/1). Lever must move freely but with resistance so that it will stay in position it is shifted to.

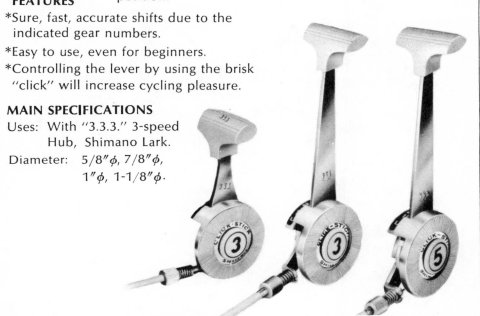

Previous levers have had a weak point in their unclear shifting positions. Click Stick has shifting positions 1, 2, 3, 4 and 5 clearly marked, so you can change accurately with the help of a light "click" sound in each position.

FEATURES

*Sure, fast, accurate shifts due to the indicated gear numbers.

*Easy to use, even for beginners.

*Controlling the lever by using the brisk "click" will increase cycling pleasure.

MAIN SPECIFICATIONS

Uses: With "3.3.3." 3-speed Hub, Shimano Lark.

Diameter: 5/8″φ, 7/8″φ, 1″φ, 1-1/8″φ.

Fig. 122.   Shimano click-stick shifting levers. To disassemble, pry number plate off with screwdriver and loosen bolt behind it. Always replace parts in the same order as when disassembling.

Fig. 123.   Shimano trigger control. This trigger control clicks into the desired gear by using the shifting lever. The red button on the lever indicates the gear you are in. To disassemble, remove screws in center and lift off the number plate. Cable can then be taken off or put on as required.

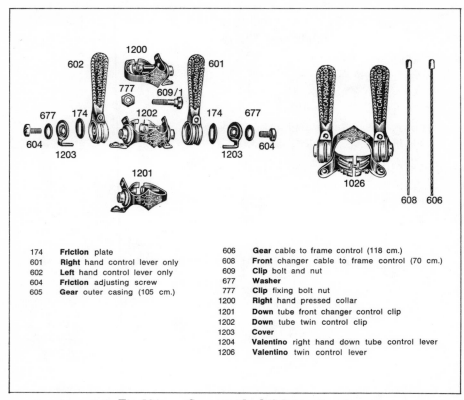

174	**Friction** plate	606	**Gear** cable to frame control (118 cm.)
601	**Right** hand control lever only	608	**Front** changer cable to frame control (70 cm.)
602	**Left** hand control lever only	609	**Clip** bolt and nut
604	**Friction** adjusting screw	677	**Washer**
605	**Gear** outer casing (105 cm.)	777	**Clip** fixing bolt nut
		1200	**Right** hand pressed collar
		1201	**Down** tube front changer control clip
		1202	**Down** tube twin control clip
		1203	**Cover**
		1204	**Valentino** right hand down tube control lever
		1206	**Valentino** twin control lever

Fig. 124.   Campagnola shift lever controls.

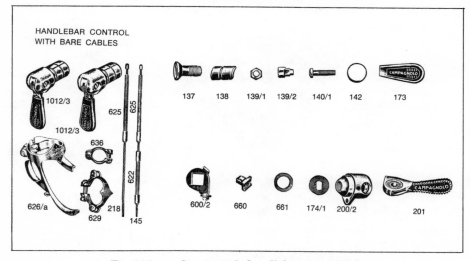

HANDLEBAR CONTROL
WITH BARE CABLES

Fig. 125.   Campagnola handlebar tip controls.

Chapter V

Crank Assemblies and Sprocket Clusters

CRANK ASSEMBLIES

There are five different types of crank assemblies that are made for bicycles. Basically they all perform the same function. The crank assembly is the means of transferring power from the bicycle rider's legs to the rear wheel. All crank assemblies have a crank housing which is the bottom bracket of the bicycle frame. The crank arms are fitted into the housing and the sprocket or sprockets are attached to them; the bicycle pedals are attached to the crank arms.

ONE-PIECE CRANK SET

The one-piece crank set is used chiefly on American-made bicycles. There is one type that is used on small children's bicycles using wheels up to 20 inches. This type crank is made of a ⅜-inch to ½-inch steel rod which is bent and has either nylon bearings or ball bearings in a sleeve that is clamped onto the frame of the bicycle. The sprocket is welded to the crank and the pedals are sleeve type that slide on the ends of the crank arms and are held in place by a fastening cap. When excessive play develops in this assembly, it is necessary to replace

117

Fig. 126.   **American type one-piece crank.**

the bearings. Keep the bearings well lubricated with machine oil for longer life.

Another type of one-piece crank is used on bicycles of all sizes, including 10-speeds. This crank is a forged crank having threads on the right side to hold the sprocket in place, and left-hand threads on the left side to fasten the adjusting cone and lock nut in place. The ends of the crank are threaded on the right side with a ½-inch x 20 right-hand thread and on the left side with a ½-inch x 20 left-hand thread.

TO DISASSEMBLE

Remove pedal on left side (opposite the sprocket) turning clockwise. Remove lock nut also turning clockwise; remove lock washer and remove adjusting cone, turning clockwise. Remove bearing and force right bearing out of cup, then remove crank from crank housing.

Fig. 127.   Bottom bracket of three-piece crank.

TO LUBRICATE

Clean out crank cups with a rag. Clean crank bearings and crank cones. Apply a coat of lightweight grease and reassemble. Be sure to place bearings on cones with open balls facing into the housing. Adjust left adjusting cone finger tight. Place lock washer into slot on crank and thread lock nut onto crank and fasten securely. Make sure that the crank spins freely without having any side play.

TWO-PIECE CRANK

The two-piece crank is used on some German and Italian bicycles. The right crank arm and axle are one piece, and the axle is threaded on the right and left side so that the sprocket can be attached and locked in place on the right side with a cone and adjusted on the left side with an adjusting cone, lock washer, and lock nut. The right side cone has right-hand threads, and the left side cone has left-hand threads. When assembling, place bearing rings in hub so that the open balls face inward. Tighten adjusting screw finger-tight and tighten lock nut securely. Lubricate bearings with a lightweight grease.

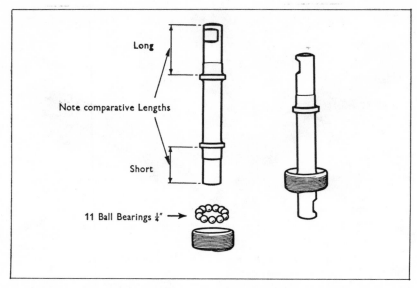

Fig. 128.   The crank axle has a longer space between the cone on the axle and the end of the axle on the right side to accommodate the sprocket(s) attached to it.

THREE-PIECE CRANK

There are two types of three-piece cranks. One is the cotter pin-type and the other is the cotterless-type. They function exactly alike. The cotterless crank is the better of the two because there is less chance of the crank arms loosening up.

THREE-PIECE CRANK (COTTER PIN-TYPE)

The crank assembly consists of an axle, two threaded crank cups, two sets of ball bearings (11 on each side), a lock nut, the right crank and sprocket, and the left crank arm. The crank cups are threaded into the crank housing and the left crank cup is locked in place with a lock nut. The crank arms are held in place on the axle by means of slotted crank cotters which are threaded on one end and tighten the crank arms to the axle when the nuts are tightened on the crank cotters.

THREE-PIECE CRANK (COTTERLESS)

The three-piece cotterless crank assembly is fitted to the bi-

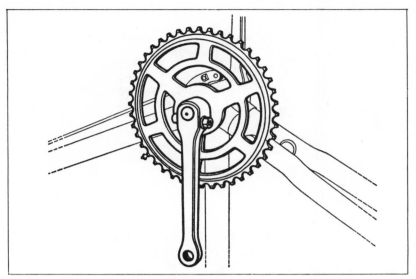

Fig. 129.   Right side crank arm with sprocket attached.

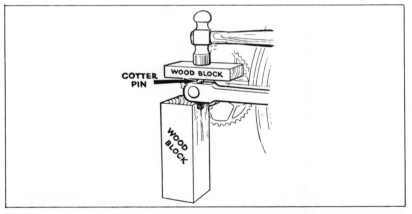

Fig. 130.   Loose cranks may be tightened by driving the cotter pin home and tightening the nut. To protect cotter, a hardwood block should be used between hammer and head of cotter. If crank is very slack, the parts should be examined and replaced if damaged.

cycle exactly the same way as the three-piece crank with cotter pins. It differs in that the ends of the axle are squared and threaded on the inside. The crank arms have square holes to fit on the axle and are held in place with bolts that screw into the ends of the crank axle.

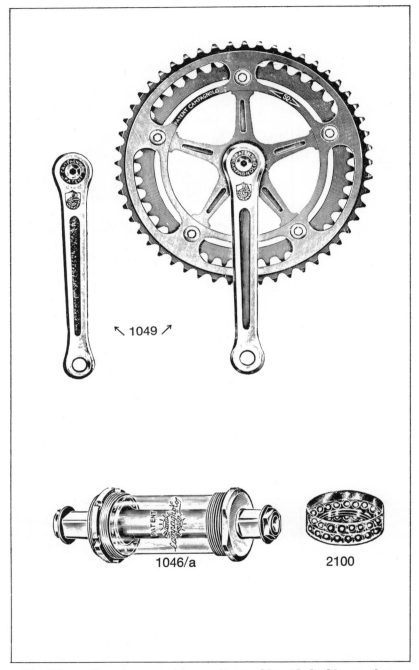

Fig. 131.   Complete cotterless crank assembly with double sprocket.

744 **Cotterless** road spindle
745 **Fixed** cup
746 **Adjustable** cup
747 **Lockring** 3,5 mm. standard size
(available also in 4 and 4,5 mm.)
748 **Fixing** screw
749 **Fixing** washer
2100 **Bottom** bracket special ball races

Fig. 132.   Cotterless axle assembly.

SPROCKET CLUSTERS

The sprocket cluster is threaded onto the hub of the rear wheel. It can consists of two to six sprockets and range from 12 teeth to 36 teeth. The smaller the sprocket, the higher the gear ratio, and the larger the sprocket, the lower the gear ratio. Some clusters are made so that the individual sprockets can be removed from the main body while others are fixed at the factory and cannot be removed.

The main body of the cluster has two sets of ball bearings in it for ease of turning. Also, two fine ratchet springs are fastened to pawls so that the sprockets will pull in one direction and free-wheel in the other. The top plate on the face of the cluster is removable (by unscrewing clockwise) for cleaning and oil-

Fig. 133.   Multiple sprocket clusters.

ing the bearings. Be careful to replace the ratchet springs and pawls in the same position when reassembling. Do not tighten the outer plate too tight, or the cluster will not spin freely.

MULTIPLE CRANK SPROCKETS

Multiple crank sprockets are used on bicycles to get a greater number of gear ratios. The sprockets are fastened to each other by means of screws and washer spacers. Figure 133 shows various multiple crank sprockets.

Chapter VI

Frame and Fork Aligning

ALIGNING A FRAME

To align a bicycle frame it is essential to have a good strong vise that is solidly affixed to a bench anchored either to the floor or to the wall. You will also need a long steel rod approximately one inch thick and three feet long (you may get an old auto rear axle at an auto wrecker), and a heavy rubber or rawhide mallet.

There are several ways that a frame will bend. Each type of bend requires a different method to straighten it again.

The most common type of bent frame is caused when the bicycle is driven into a solid object, and the horizontal tube as well as the diagonal tube from the head of the bicycle become buckled (see Fig. 134). To get this type of bend out of the frame, place the one inch steel bar in the vise so that approximately one foot of the bar is protruding in a horizontal position. After having removed the fork from the frame, but leaving the head cups in the frame, place the head of the frame into the steel bar protruding from the vise. Using the whole frame as a lever, pull the frame until the bend comes out. Sometimes, in addition to this, an assistant can rap the frame smartly at the place where it is buckled at the same time you are pulling the frame. This should put the frame back into its normal shape.

There are times when a bicycle is run over by a car, and the

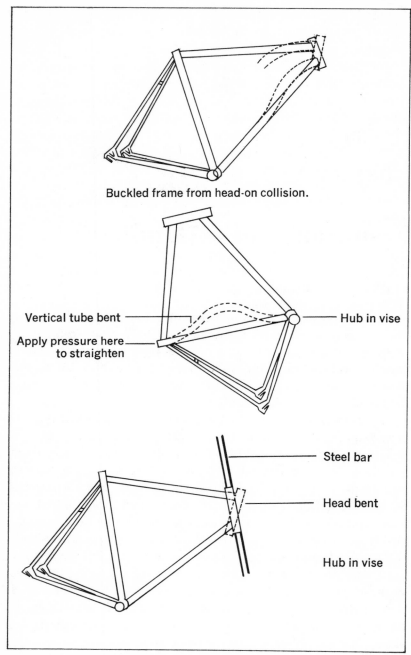

Buckled frame from head-on collision.

Vertical tube bent

Apply pressure here to straighten

Hub in vise

Steel bar

Head bent

Hub in vise

Fig. 134.   Buckled frame from head on collision, with head twisted left or right. Place hub in vise, and twist bar in head to straighten.

frame bends in such a way that the head of the bicycle is no longer perpendicular to the vertical tube of the frame directly under the seat. In this case, you must take everything off the frame except the head cups. Using the bottom bracket (crank housing) as a central point, place a yard stick (making sure that it is straight) against the side of the crank housing and direct the yard stick towards the top of the frame at the seat post. The vertical tube should be parallel to the yard stick. If is it not, then the vertical tube is bent. To straighten this tube, place the crank housing securely in the vise so that the vertical tube is in a horizontal position. If you can, place the one inch steel rod into the vertical tube, and pull on the bar until the vertical tube is straightened. If the hole in the vertical tube is too small for the steel bar, get some 12 gauge wire (old coat hangers) and wrap the steel bar securely against the vertical tube and pull the steel bar until the frame is straight.

There are times when the head of the frame becomes bent. When this happens the head is tilted at an angle to the vertical tube. You can see it by lining up the head and vertical tube with your eye. They should be parallel. To straighten the head, place the frame in the vise at the bottom bracket housing in such a position that the head is perpendicular to the bench. Then, with the cups inserted into the head, place the steel rod in the head and using as much leverage as you can, bend the frame until the head is parallel to the vertical tube.

Another bend repair must be made when the horizontal and diagonal tubes are bent either to the right or left side. This can be determined by placing the yard stick flat against the bottom bracket and leading it up to the head of the bicycle in line with the diagonal tube. The diagonal tube must be parallel to the yard stick. If it is not, then the frame is bent. To straighten this type of bend, fasten the bottom bracket in the vise so that the head is just above the top of the bench. Using your one-inch steel bar, place it between the head and the vertical tube and pull on it until frame is back to the desired position.

The rear upper stays can be straightened (if bent inwards) by laying the frame on the ground and placing a block of wood under the top of the vertical tube and another block of wood under the end of the upper stay and using a mallet on the bend. When the lower stay is bent, place the frame in the vise at the

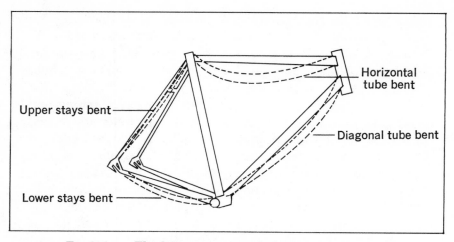

Fig. 135.   The different ways in which a frame can be bent.

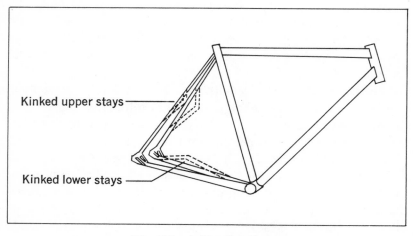

Fig. 136.   Bends in frame.

lower stay right next to the spot where the bend is. Using the frame as leverage, straighten the lower stay.

If both lower and upper rear frame stays are bent to one side, place the frame in the vise at the lower bracket housing and pull the frame back to the desired position. The rear stays are in line when they are both equally spaced from the bottom bracket housing. You can determine this by placing the yard stick flat against the bottom bracket housing and running the yardstick along the bottom rear stays. The yardstick should pass on the inside of the end of the rear stays approximately one-half inch from the frame ends. When the tops of the upper rear stays are both bent to one side, lay the frame down and, using blocks of wood under the top of the vertical tube and end of the rear stay, pound it with a mallet at the cross member that joins the two upper stays until the upper stays are in line.

A sharp kink in either of the rear stays cannot be straightened entirely, but most of it can be taken out by placing the frame in the vise at the point of the kink and closing the vise on it. If most of the kink does not come out, then place the rear stay (at the point where it is bent) on top of the closed vise and pound out the rest of the kink with a heavy hammer.

The rear stay fork openings can also be straightened out by pounding them, or squeezing them in a vise.

A kink in any of the diagonal, horizontal or vertical tubes cannot be taken out. After straightening the tube, fill in the kink with auto putty or with brass using a welding torch.

ALIGNING THE FORK

The bicycle fork will bend when the bicycle is driven into some heavy object, or at times, up or down a large curb by the street. When the fork is in line, it is perfectly balanced and the bicycle can be ridden in a balanced manner (providing the rest of the bike is not out of line). A fork can bend several different ways, and sometimes all different ways at once. The fork sides can bend backward or forward, the fork crown can bend, and the fork head can bend. For a fork to be perfectly in line, the sides have to be parallel to the head, and the head must be perpendicular to the fork crown. Also, the fork sides must be

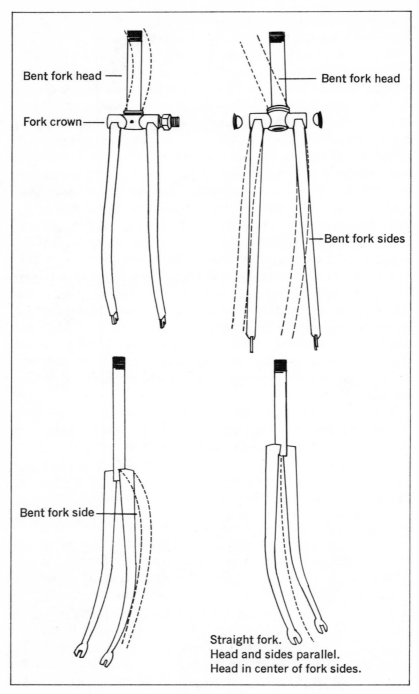

Fig. 137.   Different positions of bent forks.

straight with the fork head (see Fig. 137) at least half the distance down the sides.

A good tool to use for straightening a fork is a three foot steel rod, one inch in diameter. File a groove in one end of the rod and wrap a piece of 12 gauge wire around the rod in such a way that the wire will form an oval with the widest part approximately 4″ across. Use at least enough wire to wrap around the bar six times. To straighten one side of a fork, clamp the head of the fork in the vise and place the wire cage over the fork end. Slide the steel rod into the wire cage with the grooved end going up to the point where the fork is bent. Then pull on the steel rod until the fork bends back to the desired shape. If the fork is bent sideways so that the fork sides are not parallel to the fork head, they can be bent back into place with your hands while the fork head is in the vise. If the fork head is bent, place it in the vise up to the part where the bend begins, and using the rest of the fork as leverage you will be able to bend it back into shape. If the fork crown is bent, place the fork head in the vise up to the crown. Then, using a front wheel axle with cones and nuts, lock the axle into the fork (as if it were as a wheel), and place one end of the rod on the fork crown and the other end through the axle for leverage and pull. This should straighten the fork crown.

When the flare in the fork sides is too great, lay the fork on the ground with a wood block under the crown for support and hit the fork with a mallet at the highest point of the flare. This will lessen the flare. If there is not enough flare in the fork, hold the fork in your hand at the head, and placing the flared part of the fork side against a rounded edge on the work bench, hit the tip end of the fork with a mallet until you get the desired taper.

On a solid steel fork, when the fork sides bend, place the fork side in the vise up to the crown and, using the steel rod fitted into the fork head for leverage, pull the rod. This will return the fork side to the desired position.

To test for perfect alignment of the fork, lay the fork on the bench and place a level dowel rod across the fork crown and another rod across the fork tips. Look at the two rods in this position: they should be perfectly parallel to each other, and the fork head should be directly in the center between the fork tips.

Chapter VII

Building and Truing Wheels

BUILDING WHEELS

As there are rims with different numbers of holes in them, always make sure, when building a wheel, that the rim has the same number of spoke holes as the hub being used. Upon examining the rim, you will notice that the spoke holes are staggered. Every other hole is on the other side of the rim. The easiest way to spoke a rim is to lay one edge flat against a bench with the other resting in your lap as you sit on a chair. Place the spokes into every other hole on one side of the hub, and then thread them into the rim using the holes in the rim that are closest to the side of the hub that you have the spokes in. For example, with the hub in the center of the rim as it lies flat, the spoke holes on top are used with the spoke holes in the rim that are nearest to the top of the rim. As the spokes in the hub are placed into every other hole on top of the hub, you also must place these spokes into the top holes of the rim, every other top hole. Assuming that you are building a wheel with 36 spokes, you will have nine spokes in the hub and in the rim. Turn the spoke nipples on to the spokes about two turns. After the nine spokes are in place, put one spoke into the same side of the hub, except put it in upside down (reversed with respect to the first nine spokes). Then, twisting the hub with your hand until all the spokes tighten up on the rim, place the tenth spoke across the

other spokes until the end just reaches the inside edge of the rim
at a hole that is also on top of the rim. You will be crossing
either three or four spokes, depending on the size of the spokes
that you use. Turn the spoke nipple on to the spoke two turns.
Place eight more spokes into the hub and tighten them two
turns onto the rim in sequence with the 10th spoke. Turn the
wheel upside down and place the 19th spoke into any hole in
the hub from the top. Lead the spoke on a tangent to the hub
until the end of the spoke just touches the inside of the rim and
place the spoke nipple on it, turning the nipple two turns. While
finding the right hole for the 19th spoke, if you put the spoke
in the wrong hole it will stick through the rim too far, or else it
will be a little too short for that hole. It is important that the
spoke fits exactly into the right hole. Then put the 20th through
the 27th spokes in sequence into the hub and into the rim,
following the 19th spoke. The 28th spoke is put into the hub
from the underside and crosses over the same number of spokes
as on the first 18. Place the rest of the spokes in the hub in
sequence and tighten them all two turns, as on the other spokes.
Now that all the spokes are in the hub and the rim, start with
the first spoke next to the valve stem hole in the rim and tighten
all the spokes two turns. Continue tightening them two or three
turns each until all the spokes are tight. Always make sure that
you do not tighten some spokes more than others, as this will
make the wheel oval shaped. When all the spokes are tight, the
wheel must be "trued." That means the spokes have to be adjusted so that there will be no wobble in the wheel. Place the
wheel in the fork of a bicycle, or if a back wheel, in the rear
stays of the bicycle, and spin the wheel. While the wheel is turning, hold your thumb close to the rim edge and see if the wheel
has any wobble. If most of the rim edge comes close to your
thumb, and there is a spot on the rim that is away from your
thumb, loosen the spokes two turns on the opposite side of the
rim from your thumb, and tighten the spokes on the same side
as the thumb. This will draw the rim closer to your thumb. If,
while spinning the wheel, most of the rim misses your thumb,
but one spot touches it, loosen the spokes about two turns at the
place where it touches your thumb, and tighten the spokes on
the opposite side. In this way you should be able to get the
wheel perfectly straight.

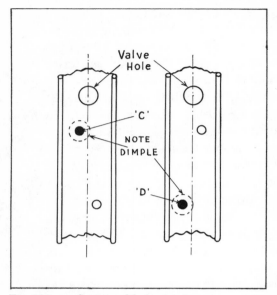

Fig. 138.   Staggered holes in rim.

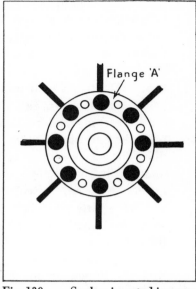

Fig. 139.   Spokes inserted in every other hole.

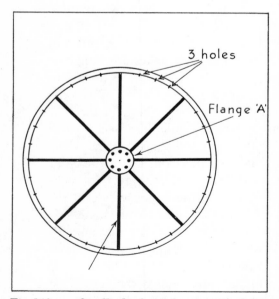

Fig. 140.   On all wheels, spokes are placed in every fifth hole in the rim.

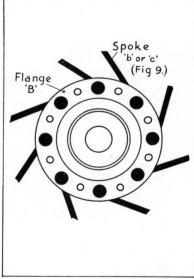

Fig. 141.   Spokes run almost on a tangent to hub.

BUILDING REAR WHEELS FOR DERAILLEUR HUBS

When building wheels that are to be used with derailleurs, follow the same procedure as above except that after you have placed all the spokes into the hub and the rim, tighten the spokes that are on the cluster side of the hub three turns each before you proceed to tighten the spokes as explained above. This will make the hub off-center so that the addition of the cluster of sprockets will not make the wheel ride to one side of the bicycle frame.

STRAIGHTENING THE WHEEL

There are many ways that a wheel will bend. Most of the time, a bent wheel is caused by broken spokes. A wheel will bend if the spokes are loose, and it will also bend if you run it into some heavy object, or up or down a curb. A wheel can have just a simple bend in it, or it can be "sprung"; it can have a hop in it, or it can be dented at the rim edge. I shall take each type of bend separately and explain how to straighten it.

SIMPLE BEND

A simple bend will cause a wheel to weave from side to side if it is ¼" or less off-center. This type of bend can be straightened by loosening and tightening spokes. If there are spokes missing or broken, be sure to replace them with the same length spoke as the others in the wheel. Watch how the spokes are placed in the rim and be sure to follow the sequence of the other spokes. To straighten the wheel (if you can replace the spokes without taking the wheel off the bike) turn the bicycle over and spin the wheel. Holding your hand against the frame of the bike, use your thumb as a guide and find the place where the wheel is bent. Loosen the spokes directly across the rim from where your thumb shows the wheel to be bent. Tighten the spokes at the point where there is too much room between your thumb and the rim. This will draw the rim closer to your thumb. If the rim hits your thumb at one place and the rest of the rim misses, then loosen the spokes at that point, and tighten the spokes directly across from where it touches. In this way, the wheel will straighten out.

LOOSE SPOKES

When a wheel is bent because the spokes are loose, first tighten all the spokes. Starting at the valve stem hole on the rim, tighten them all one or two turns depending on how loose they are. Always make sure that you tighten all the spokes to prevent getting a "hop" in the wheel. After all the spokes are tight, check the rim with your thumb, and you will be able to make the wheel straight by loosening the spokes that are too close to your thumb and tightening the ones on the other side, or the other way around if part of the rim is too far from your thumb.

SPRUNG WHEEL

On a sprung wheel the rim is bent so badly that it will rub against the frame on both sides at different parts of the rim. If you have this type of bend in the rim, remove the wheel from the bicycle and remove the tire and tube. Loosen all the spokes approximately three turns. After turning the wheel a few times, determine where it is bent the most, and draw up the spokes as tight as you can on the side that is furthest away from center so that the rim will try to return to its original shape. If this does not spring the rim back to shape, then lay the rim on a bench so that the bent-out part overlaps the bench. Then pound this part of the wheel with a mallet. This will usually cause the wheel to go back close to the right shape. This method can be used on any wheel that is too far out of "true." After the rim is forced back to its approximate shape by using this method, you will be able to finish the job by loosening and tightening spokes.

HOP IN WHEEL

When a wheel has a "hop" in it, it is usually caused by the spokes being incorrectly tightened. If the spokes are tightened more on one part of a wheel than another, it will cause the wheel to be shaped in such a way that one part of the rim is closer to the hub and another part further away. This makes the wheel hop. To correct this condition, loosen all the spokes until you see the end of the thread on the spokes, and therefore know that they are threaded equally into the nipples. Then tighten the spokes making sure that you turn each nipple the same amount. Start with two turns on each, then one turn all the way around, and continue until all the spokes are tight. This will take the hop out of the wheel. Then proceed to straighten it for side clearance.

DENTS IN THE RIM

Dents in the rim are caused when the wheel hits a curb or other raised object on the street. To remove these dents, hold a heavy weight against one side of the rim opposite the dent, and use a hammer to give the rim a sharp blow at the spot where it is dented. This procedure will put the rim back into its original shape. If the rim is dented inward, remove the tire and tube, and using heavy pliers you will be able to bend it back into place.

Chapter VIII

Short Cuts on Common Repairs

FLAT TIRES

The most common repair on a bicycle is a flat tire. Much time can be saved in repairing it if you follow this simple procedure.

Without removing the wheel from the bicycle, fill the tire with air.

Listen for the sound of air escaping from the tire.

Using tire tools, remove the portion of the tire from the rim where the air is escaping.

Patch the tube and replace the tube and tire on the wheel and fill with air.

GEARS SLIP ON A THREE-SPEED BICYCLE

This is a common occurrence with a three-speed bicycle. To correct, follow this procedure:

Check the gear cable for slack in third gear.

Take up slack by adjusting at end of cable where it attaches to actuating chain.

If cable cannot be adjusted at adjusting barrel, slack can be taken out at the clamp holding the cable to the frame.

Loosen clamp and slide along frame until all slack is removed from cable while it is in third gear. Tighten clamp.

HAND BRAKES TOO HARD TO SQUEEZE, OR DO NOT RELEASE

Tight adjustment on the hand brake levers, or frayed or rusty cables will cause hand brakes to be too hard to squeeze or to bind.

Remove inner cable cores from cable housings and grease them. Replace in same position.

Loosen adjusting screw on brake handle.

Loosen double nut on brake carriage. Tighten outer nut while inner nut is loose.

CHAIN MAKES GRINDING NOISE

Check tension of chain. Holding chain in your fingers half-way between front and rear sprockets, chain should be able to move up and down about one inch.

To loosen chain, loosen axle nut on rear wheel and give the chain the desired amount of slack.

When tightening axle nut, make sure that wheel is in center of frame.

WHEELS DO NOT ROLL FREELY

Lift front end of bicycle off ground and spin the wheel slowly. Wheel must turn continuously several revolutions before stopping. If it binds, loosen one axle nut of the front wheel and loosen the axle adjusting cone with a flat wrench just enough to cause the wheel to spin freely. Tighten axle nut.

If rear wheel does not spin freely, loosen the adjusting cone on either the right or left side, depending on where it is. Tighten outer nut and check wheel for side play. If there is side play, tighten cone a little more.

CRANK DOES NOT SPIN FREELY

Loosen crank lock nut and loosen crank adjusting cone. Be sure that you do not loosen the adjusting cone so much that you will have side play in the crank. Tighten lock nut.

BICYCLE FORK HAS UP AND DOWN PLAY

Head lock nut and cone are loose. Tighten fork adjusting cone finger tight, and tighten fork lock nut against it.

PEDAL CRANK HITS FRAME

Crank arm is bent, or crank assembly is loose.

If crank assembly is loose, you will be able to feel it by shaking it with your hand. If loose, first check the right-hand cone. It must be tight. If loose, use a punch and hammer to tighten it. If tight, loosen lock nut on left side and tighten the adjusting cone finger tight, and tighten lock nut with punch and hammer.

If crank arm is bent, remove pedal and place a length of pipe over the crank arm and pull back to shape.

HANDLEBAR STEM WORN, CAUSING HANDLEBAR TO MOVE UP AND DOWN

Remove handlebar stem from bicycle, and remove handlebar from stem. File or cut a ⅛-inch section off of stem where binder bolt clamps it together. This will allow the stem to tighten against the handlebar.

HANDLEBAR STEM FROZEN IN PLACE SO THAT YOU CANNOT REMOVE IT FROM BICYCLE

A stem becomes frozen either because it is rusted in place or it is broken inside the fork. First loosen the stem bolt approximately ¼ inch on the stem. Using a hammer tap the bolt down. This will loosen the binder bolt inside the fork. If you still cannot remove the stem by twisting and pulling on the handlebar, then remove the stem bolt completely and after pouring some light lubricant or kerosene between the stem and the fork, give the stem several sharp blows on the underside of the stem. This will force it out of the fork.

SADDLE MOVES BACK AND FORTH; WILL NOT TIGHTEN

Replace saddle clamps. Serrations are worn.

CHAIN COMES OFF SPROCKET

Remove chain and spin crank, watching for bent sprocket. If sprocket is bent, you can hammer it until it spins straight.

If sprocket is straight, check frame alignment. Place a straight edge against crank sprocket and see that it leads straight back to the rear sprocket. If not, follow frame alignment procedure in other chapter.

On a five- or ten-speed bicycle, a straight edge should come in line with the third sprocket on the cluster.

CHAIN STICKS ON LARGE CRANK SPROCKET OF TEN SPEED

Many times, a chain will not drop down to the smaller sprocket when shifted, but will hang up between the sprocket and frame of the bicycle. When this happens, it is because there are some rough teeth on the large sprocket which do not allow the chain to come off it when shifted. Using a flat file, file the sprocket teeth until they are smooth.

HAND BRAKES SQUEAL WHEN BRAKE IS APPLIED

This condition happens occasionally on new bicycles. To stop the squealing, remove the brake shoes and brake rubbers and file them down until a new surface appears. If brakes continue to squeal, replace the brake rubbers with new ones.

BRAKE ARM JUMPS WHEN COASTER BRAKE IS APPLIED

This can cause serious damage to the coaster brake. To correct it, remove wheel from the bicycle and tighten the brake arm lock nut with a crescent wrench. Be careful to keep the brake arm adjusted loose enough so that the wheel spins freely, and at the same time there is no side play.

SIDE PULL BRAKES ARE NOT CENTERED

This condition happens frequently when the brake spring is set a little off-center. To center the brake shoes, place a screw driver on top of the brake spring on the side where the brake is furthest from the wheel. Tap the screw driver sharply with a hammer until the brake blocks center themselves in relation to the wheel.

REMOVING TIGHT CRANK PINS FROM A THREE-PIECE CRANK

To remove a tight crank pin it is necessary to hold a weight underneath the crank arm, and after removing the crank pin nut, tap the crank pin sharply with a hammer until it comes loose.

DATE DUE